WITHDRAWN
HARVARD LIBRARY
WITHDRAWN

A FIFTEENTH-CENTURY FRANCISCAN FRENCH OFFICE
Translation and Commentary of the
Hours of the Passion

Heures de la Passion. English + French (Middle French)

A FIFTEENTH-CENTURY FRANCISCAN FRENCH OFFICE
Translation and Commentary of the
Hours of the Passion

Nicole Crossley-Holland

Mediaeval Studies
Volume 4

The Edwin Mellen Press
Lewiston/Queenston/Lampeter

Library of Congress Cataloging-in-Publication Data

Heures de la Passion. English & French (Middle French)
  A fifteenth century Franciscan French office : translation and commentary on the "Hours of the Passion" / [by] Nicole Crossley-Holland.
    p.   cm. -- (Mediaeval studies ; v. 4)
  Text of the Middle French poem Heures de la Passion, published from Boston Public Library manuscript 1551 (where it has variant title La Passion de Nostre Seigneur), together with an English translation and commentary.
  Includes bibliographical references.
  ISBN 0-88946-268-2
  1. Jesus Christ--Passion--Poetry. 2. Christian poetry, French--Translations into English. 3. Christian poetry, English--Translations from French. I. Crossley-Holland, Nicole. II. Catholic Church. III. Boston Public Library. Manuscript. 1551. IV. Title. V. Series: Mediaeval studies (Lewiston, N. Y.) ; v. 4.
PQ1561.H4513 1990
841'.3--dc20   90-31511
                                                                CIP

This is volume 4 in the continuing series
Mediaeval Studies
Volume 4 ISBN 0-88946-268-2
MS Series ISBN 0-88946-264-X

A CIP catalog record for this book
is available from the British Library.

Copyright © 1991 The Edwin Mellen Press

All rights reserved. For information contact

The Edwin Mellen Press   The Edwin Mellen Press
       Box 450   Box 67
  Lewiston, New York   Queenston, Ontario
      USA 14092   CANADA L0S 1L0

The Edwin Mellen Press, Ltd.
Lampeter, Dyfed, Wales
UNITED KINGDOM SA48 7DY

Printed in the United States of America

To
Peter Crossley-Holland,
*whose inspiration and support over the years
have helped beyond measure*

TABLE OF CONTENTS

List of plates and illustrations i
Acknowledgements iii
Preface v
Introduction vii

Part I
The Hours of the Passion

The Text 3
The Translation 21

Part II
Critical Commentary

Description and history of the manuscripts 29
Principles and method of editing 37
Prosodic and linguistic aspects 49
Sources and commentaries 69
Liturgical use 99
The miniatures of the Boston manuscript 121

Appendices

    A. The two additional stanzas in the Boston manuscript 161
    B. Examples of double tercet in pentasyllabic lines in late mediaeval French literature 163
    C. The *Via Sacra* text 169
    D. The *Canticum Passionis* 173
    E. The *Canticum Pindaricum loco Te Deum* and the *Ode Saphica* [sic] *ad Divam Catharinam* 179

Plates and illustrations 181
Bibliography 197
Index Nominum 205

LIST OF PLATES

I.	Boston Public Library Ms. 129:	The Binding	183
II.	" " " " " :	The Betrayal in the Garden of Gethsemane	184
III.	" " " " " :	Jesus Before Pilate	185
IV.	" " " " " :	The Scourging of Jesus	186
V.	" " " " " :	Jesus Carrying his Cross	187
VI.	" " " " " :	Jesus dies on the Cross	188
VII.	" " " " " :	The Descent from the Cross	189
VIII.	" " " " " :	The Entombment	190

Reproduced by courtesy of the Trustees of the Boston Public Library

IX.	Walters Art Gallery Ms. 439 fol. 28.	191

*Reproduced by courtesy of the
Trustees of the Walters Art Gallery Baltimore*

LIST OF ILLUSTRATIONS

The illustrations were drawn by Frances C. Wright

I.	Young Heads	192
II.	Old Heads	192
III.	Feet (round)	192
IV.	Feet (pointed)	193
V.	Feet: Collection Dutuit Ms. 456	193
VI.	Figures	194
VII.	Weapons	195
VIII.	Trees	196
IX.	Gestures	196
X.	Signature	196

ACKNOWLEDGEMENTS

I wish to thank the various organizations and persons who have helped me, and first, the National Endowment for the Humanities of the United States of America which granted me a generous Fellowship towards carrying out this project. I also wish to thank the staff of the Institute of Historical Research, University of London; of the New York Public Library; and of the Research Library at the University of California, Los Angeles, for the facilities placed at my disposal. I am grateful to Viscount Coke who allowed me to peruse the manuscripts in his private collection at Holkham Hall, Norfolk. For their active interest and personal help, I wish to thank particularly : Dr. John Plummer (Pierpont Morgan Library, New York); Prof. Robert Calkins (Cornell University); Dr. Lilian Randall (Walters Art Gallery, Baltimore); Prof. Carl Lofmark (University of Wales); last but not least, my husband, Prof. Peter Crossley-Holland (Universities of California and Wales.)

The generous assistance of the Pantyfedwen Fund of Saint David's University College Lampeter in the printing of this work is acknowledged here.

PREFACE

The scholarly distinction of the Boston Public Library is well known. It can boast of several remarkable collections such as the Barton, Bowditch, Prince and Ticknor; and one of its greatest benefactors, Josiah H. Benton, bequeathed to this library his important collection of Books of Common Prayer. More recently, in 1931, the Franciscan collection belonging to Paul Sabatier entered the Boston Public Library. Consisting of three manuscripts, 1735 printed books and 638 pamphlets, it is probably, by its sheer bulk and also by the variety of material it offers, one of the most important Franciscan collections extant.

In 1954, thanks to the Josiah H. Benton fund, the Department of Rare Books and Manuscripts of the Boston Public Library acquired from the London book-dealer Maggs a slender and exquisite fifteenth-century manuscript (accession number 1551= med.129). It was my good fortune, several years ago, to happen upon this manuscript, and I soon came to realize that the library had acquired a work of very great importance, both artistically and liturgically. It contains a poem in French on the Passion of Our Lord and displays seven superb miniatures in *grisaille*. I was able to establish the textual and liturgical connexion with the Franciscan Order, thus rendering the presence of this manuscript in the Boston Public Library of even greater moment than I had at first thought, since it sheds especial lustre on the library's extensive Franciscan holdings from the Sabatier collection.

I think I have carried the research as far as is possible on the strength of the evidence at present available. Even when it has not been possible to solve certain problems, I have nonetheless stated them for the benefit of further researchers in the hope that these problems may, some time, find a solution.

INTRODUCTION

The *Passionale* presented here commends itself to the attention of mediaevalists. It is not only that its prosodic form and unusual divisions invite attention, but one also sees a definite sense of purpose which emerges on better acquaintance with the text. In this respect, it far outreaches texts of a comparable nature.

This prevalent sense of purpose impelled me to search for the key. I decided to study this *Passion* in all its aspects: palaeographical and codicological, linguistic, theological, liturgical and artistic, as I realised that only a study taking all types of evidence into account could do justice to it and could help recover the fullness of the meaning it held when it was created. So often, documents which represent the fruits of work in several disciplines are studied under but a single aspect. At best, the result is misleading; at worst, general conclusions drawn from this single aspect can hopelessly distort one's perspective. Working from a fragmentary approach indeed incurs the risk of serious misrepresentation. A work of art conceived in many aspects and on many levels should be studied in all these ways, so that the body of unbiased evidence may be so presented as to reveal all possible converging elements and their interconnexions. This is why I have adopted a holistic approach to this study, as the only one capable of bringing to light the true meaning and strength of our *Passion*.

I also feel that in the study of such documents, a scholar should endeavour to contribute to the wider knowledge of the period in which it was produced. Thus it is necessary to place the documents in the perspective of a wide collection of data from comparable sources. This I have also tried to do.

The results bear out the method. Taking into consideration its date of composition and place of origin, this *Passionale* finds its place in the literature of *devotio moderna*. Its monastic appurtenance *in that form* makes it a unique document on certain aspects of Franciscan spirituality as well as monastic and para-liturgical practice; whilst palaeographical and artistic data make it possible to date the Boston manuscript within two years.

The text, which evokes the events of the Passion from the Last Supper to the Burial of Jesus, is a poem of eighty stanzas divided into sections corresponding to the Canonical Hours. I have attempted to render in my translation the simplicity and, at the same time, the forcefulness which, in the author's work, are constantly present in retelling the suffering of Christ and His mother.

We know of three manuscripts in which the *Passion* has come down to us. The first, from the Boston Public Library, with its miniatures in *grisaille*, is the only text in the volume as bound. The second manuscript, from the Bibiothèque Nationale, was part of the library of Louis de Bruges. Besides the *Passion*, it contains various other devotional treatises in the line of the *devotio moderna*, by Jean Gerson and Jean Trousseau and one imitated from Saint Bonaventure. The third manuscript is kept at the Musée Condé at Chantilly. Its history is virtually unknown. Besides the *Passion* it contains five devotional pieces in honour of Our Lady.

In comparing the texts of the three manuscripts for the purpose of critical edition, I have followed the principles and methods advocated by Dom Jacques Froger, O.S.B., and which I have applied in several of my previous editions of texts. It will be seen that this method goes far beyond the reference made to it by Foulet and Speer in 1979.[1] It appears that none of the manuscripts extant is the ancestor, but that the Boston text is closest to it. The *apparatus criticus* is positive and thoroughly repertoried, thus making it easy to use at all times.

The text is, consistently, in pentasyllabic six-line stanzas which, in fact, are double tercets rhyming aab/aab. The syllabic count reveals some interesting uses of diphthongs and rhymes. Morphology, syntax and vocabulary show Picard and Walloon influences in a text which originated in Flanders (Bruges). Anomalous though this may seem, under the dukes of Burgundy, Flemish cities acquired, through literary and artistic crosscurrents, a cosmopolitanism unusual in its day.

A study of the sources for this text--which remains anonymous--reveals a deliberate inclination towards a practical and personal understanding of the suffering of Christ. In accordance with Franciscan spirituality, the Saviour is viewed as a personal friend and a brother. But this trend goes further and bears the hallmark of the *devotio moderna*. As E. Moreau puts it: "La dévotion moderne substitue au Théocentrisme, le Christocentrisme. Elle organise la prière systématique qui se répandra dans l'Eglise Catholique et restera la forme de prière la plus usitée."[2] This "modern devotion" had been flourishing in the Netherlands and in Flanders since the late 1300s. The *Passion* edited here falls obviously within the sphere of devotion of the Brothers and Sisters of Common Life.

The format of the text bears the imprint of liturgical use, divided up as it is in sections corresponding to the Canonical Hours. The long poem was, in fact, structured to be used by Franciscan lay-brothers in place of the recitation of the Divine Office by Choir-monks. When comparing this text with other para-liturgical offices from the Dominican and Franciscan traditions, it becomes obvious that it has its place in a well-established tradition, both parochial and monastic.[3]

Of the existing manuscripts, only the Boston exemplar displays miniatures, and these are seven in all. They show a Netherlandish influence tempered with Flemish characteristics. Composition, style and techniques, all three point to the workshop of Guillaume Vrelant. Various other elements would seem to indicate a date of manufacture between 1467 and 1469. There is a strong likelihood that the artist was Alexandre Fraet.

Various appendices, figures and illustrations, as well as reproductions of this and another manuscript help to confirm the results described above.

Quite apart from its moving beauty, this *Passion* lends real weight to Francis Rapp's view of fifteenth-century spirituality: "La spiritualité du 15e. siècle, essentiellement christocentrique, s'est attachée surtout à susciter et à raviver la ferveur. Elle a permis aux partisans de la stricte observance d'infuser aux communautés réformées un courage neuf. Des ilôts de foi vivante ont donc pu se maintenir au milieu d'une chrétienté sollicitée par le laxisme et par le doute".[4]

NOTES

1   A. Foulet and M. B. Speer: *On Editing Old French Texts*. R. P. K. Lawrence, 1979. See pp. 25/26.

2   E. Moreau: *Histoire de l'Eglise en Belgique*, vol. IV Bruxelles, 1947; livre 6: "Spiritualité, piété et dévotion". See p. 358.

3   See Alessandro de Ripabottoni: *I fratelli laici nel primo ordine francescano*. Rome, 1956; pp. 276 ff.

4   Francis Rapp: "FRANCE: le 15e. siècle", col. 894/895 in M. Viller (ed.) *Dictionnaire de Spiritualité* Paris (Beauchesne), 1953.

PART I

THE HOURS OF THE PASSION

Text and Translation

LA PASSION DE NOSTRE SEIGNEUR

1. Pour mal eviter
   Et excerciter
   En bien ses pensees
   Ces choses au cler
   Qu'ay voulu ditter
   Soyent medittées.

2. C'est vraie oroison
   De la Passion
   Des[1]* principaulx poins
   Ausquelz seroit bon
   Par vraye union
   Estre uny et joins.

A MATINES

3. A la cene yras
   Ou tu trouveras
   Ton Seigneur assis
   Et depuis ce pas
   Tu contempleras
   Ses fais et ses diz.

---

* The *apparatus criticus* is to found on p. 44 ff.

4. Regarde pecheur
Comment ton Seigneur
S'est humiliez
De tant humble cuer
Comme serviteur[2]
Il lave les piez.

5. Son corps uniement
Et sang proprement
Beneist et sacra;
Ce saint sacrement
Pour no sauvement
Il institua.

6. Ce sainct sacrifice
Par grant benefice
Sacra pain et vin
Eulx estant propice
En aprist l'office
Tres hault et divin.

7. Puis apres la cene
Ses disciples maine
Envers le jardin
Parlant de la paine
Qu'a luy est prochaine[3]
Durant le chemin.

8. Il les enseigna
Et les enhorta
D'eulx mettre en priere
Puis d'eulx s'eslonga
Avec lui mena
Jehan, Jacque et Piere.[4]

9. Ausquelz dist: "Orez[5]
   Affin que n'entrez
   En temptacion".
   Puis d'un autre lez
   Est tout seul alez
   En devotion.[6]

10. Deux fois s'est transmis[7]
    Vers ses trois amis
    Qu'entour lui estoient.
    Il les a surpris
    Et tres bien repris[8]
    De ce qu'ilz dormoient.

11. En son cuer pesa[9]
    Et incorpora
    Sa grant Passion
    Dont son corps sua
    Sang qui lui coula
    Jusquez au talon.

12. Pensez bien comment
    Tres reveramment
    L'angele conforte
    Jhesus humblement
    Et benignement
    Le rechoit et porte.

13. Or oste[10] Jhesus[11]
    De sa face jus
    Le sang qu'ot sué[12]
    Puis s'en est venus
    A ses trois esleus
    Qu'a dormant trouvé.[13]

14. Il les esveilla
    Et si leur nonca
    Qu'on vint pour le prendre[14]
    Point ne se mua[15]
    Mais de fait s'en va
    Aux felons soy rendre.[16]

15. Judas le meschant
    S'en va[17] tout devant
    Jhesus embracier
    Et en demonstrant
    Trayson moult grant
    Il le va baisier.

16. Tous[18] ont cuer failly
    N'y eut si[19] hardy
    Qui fust sy[20] osez
    De toucher[21] a lui
    Dont fut esbahy
    Judas n'en doubtez.

17. "Dittes lequel c'est
    Que querrez de fait,"
    Dist nostre refuge.
    "C'est de Nazaret".
    Jhesus lors attrait
    Leur a dit: "Ce suis je".

18. A oyr sa voix
    Tous ces maleois
    Sont cheus pasmez
    Ainsi par deux fois
    Le doulz roy des roys
    Les a relevéz.

19. Juis eurent peur
    Pierre reprint cuer
    Sol coutel tyra
    Sans quelque cremeur
    Dont au serviteur
    l'oreille trencha.

20. Jhesus l'a reprise
    En son lieu remise
    Et tres bien sané.
    Lors se fait[22] la[23] prise
    He Dieu, quele emprise
    De peuple dampné.

21. Prins et lyé l'ont
    Puis entour lui font
    Huans tous ensemble
    Grief tourment lui font
    Et ainsi s'en vont
    A la maison Anne.

22. La fut buffiéz
    Et moult laidengiéz
    D'un mauvais garson
    Et fut renvoyéz
    Batus et chassiéz[24]
    Hors de la maison.

23. Ensement Annas
    Lyé col et bras
    Son Seigneur envoye
    Qu'ot livré[25] Judas
    Au grant Cayphas[26]
    Qui n'en eut[27] grant joye.

24. Si tost qu'il le vist
    Ou siege s'assist[28]
    Et puis l'interrogue.
    Quant Jhesus l'oyt
    Le vray lui a dit
    Sans longue prologue.

25. Adonc veissiez
    Ces Juis courchiéz
    Et demener fort
    Qui comme enragiéz
    Se sont escriéz
    "Dignes est de mort".

26. Ces perverses gens
    Comme hors du sens
    Ont en celle place
    De leurs crachemens
    Sales et pulens
    Couverte sa face.

A LAUDES

27. Ces mechans chetis
    Ont Jhesus assis
    Les yeulx tous bendez
    Autour se sont mis
    Eulx cinq ou eulx six
    Ferant de tous lez.

28. Disans sans faintise:
    "Or nous prophetise
    Qui cy[29] t'a feru"
    La l'ont par mainmise
    En diverse guise
    Touchié et batu.

29. Au tres amoureux
    Vont tirant les peulx
    Hors de son menton
    Mos injurieux
    Vilains et honteux
    Sur lui imposon.

30. Cy sont averis
    Les mos que tu dis
    Le soir a la cene
    C'est que scandelis
    Seront tes amis
    En la nuit prochaine.

31. Ilz s'en sont fuiz[30]
    Com tous esbahis
    Et tu ez tout seuls[31]
    Entre ces[32] rabis
    Comme les brebis[33]
    Sont entre les leups.[34]

A PRIME

32. Tout au plus matin
    Le Roy tout divin
    Ont ilz emmené
    A Pylate affin
    Que le mette a fin[35]
    Et l'ont accusé.

33. Avisez comment
    Jhesus faussement
    Cy accusé ont.[36]
    A l'accusement
    Le vray Innocent
    Bien pou y respont.

34. Jhesus vont menant
    Sacquant et boutant[37]
    Vers le roy Herode
    Qui tout maintenant
    Est venus avant
    Et a luy s'aborde.

35. Moult for l'enquesta
    Et lui demanda
    Ce que savoir volt
    Mais a tout cela
    Jhesus ne lui a
    Respondu un mot.[38]

36. Quant Herode voit
    Que mot ne disoit
    Il rescout[39] son col
    De lui se gabboit
    Et le reputoit
    Estre pour un fol.

37. Desguisement[40]
    Un blanc vestement
    Revestir lui font[41]
    Tel que fole gent[42]
    Coustumierement
    Portoient adont.

38. Par derrision
    Ainsi mené ont[43]
    Jhesus a Pylate.
    Regarde quel don
    Comment le tout bon
    Nostre amoure achate.[44]

A TIERCE

39. Regarde Jhesus
    Des faulz malostrus
    Tout nud despouillié
    A l'estache nuds
    Dessoubz et dessus
    Ont[45] tres fort lyé.

40. Tant l'ont sans pitié
    Batu et frappé
    De fouets crueux
    Et par mauvaistie
    Playé et navré
    Son corps precieux.

41. En ce piteux pas
    Ailleurs ne soit pas
    Ta pensée ouverte
    Ains regarde embas
    De son sang verras
    La terre couverte.

42. Par gab ou revel
    De pourpre un mantel
    Vont a son col metre
    Ou poing de l'aignel
    Ont mis un rosel
    En guise de sceptre.

43. Tu pues regarder
    Ton Dieu couronner
    D'espines crueuses
    Que pour toy sauver
    Tant voult endurer
    Paines angoisseuses.

44. Juys pues veoir
    Les genoulx flechir
    Et le saluer
    Sur son chief ferir
    Sang en faire issir
    Perchier et trauer.

45. Pylatte leur maine
    Eulx monstrant sa paine
    Qu'atant leur suffice
    Mais la gent vilaine
    Crie[46] a voix hautaine:
    "On le crucifie".

A MIDY

46. Considere et pense
    La dure sentence
    Crueuse et injuste
    Par quoy on offense
    La haulte clemence:
    Ton Dieu vray et juste.

47. Ilz le devestirent
    Et le revestirent
    De ses vestemens
    Grant doleur lui firent
    Mais pou en sentirent
    Selon que je sens.

48. Couronnéz, playéz
De la croix chargiéz
Est nostre exemplaire
Durement traittiéz
Boutéz et sacquiéz
Au mont de Calvaire.

49. Ta croix ne pouvoies
Tant foibles estoies
Jusqu'au[47] mont porter
Pour ce qu'en tes voies
Ta mere veoies
Tel dueil endurer.[48]

50. Quant on[49] devestoit[50]
L'abit qui tenoit
A ses dignes plaies
Tout son corps saignoit
Chascun tenir doit
Ces paroles vraies.

51. Celle au cuer courchié
A tant tournoié
Sacquié et bouté
Qu'a d'un coeuvrechie
Couvert et muchié
Son humanite.

52. Regarde Jhesus
Sur la croix pendus
Les membres tirer
Tant fort estendus
Et de cloux agus
Piez et mains cloer.

A NONE

53. Pour plus diffamer
    Le vont eslever
    Entre deux larrons
    Ce fait mediter
    Devons sans cesser
    Se nous sommes bons.

54. Son corps qui pesoit
    Les treus agrangoit
    De ses piez et mains
    Du sang qu'en yssoit[51]
    Et aval couloit
    Le mont[52] en est tains.

55. Mechans et parceux[53]
    Sont et maleureux
    Ceulx qui se deffient
    De Dieu tant piteux
    Qui prie pour ceulx
    Qui le crucifient.

56. Il estoit scitifs
    Des tres grans[54] proffis
    De l'humain lynage
    Mais ces faulx Juys
    A sa bouche ont mis
    Tres amer buvrage.

57. Hellas considere
    La paine et misere
    Et l'angoisse grande
    Qu'a ton Dieu, ton frere,
    Qui a Dieu le Pere
    Son ame commande.

58. Angoisseusement
    Son esperit rend
    Clamant de voix forte
    Lequel prestement
    En enfer descend
    Ou rompy la porte.

59. En ce lieu trouva
    Les sains qu'il ama
    De parfaicte amour.
    Il les consola
    Et la demoura
    Jusques au tiers jour.

A VESPRES

60. Quant Jhesus fina
    Soleil eclipsa
    Les pierres fendirent
    La terre trembla
    Dont de ce fait la
    Pluiseurs s'esbahirent.

61. De ce sainct Denis[55]
    Moult loing du pays
    Si prophetisa
    Choses dont depuis
    Par son bon avis
    Il se baptisa.

62. O[56] Vierge Marie
    Tu fus moult marrie
    Au pied de la croix
    Du sang ez mouillié
    Du doulx fruit de vie
    Qui est roy des roys.

63. Tendrement plourant
    Vois sur ton enfant
    Qu'en croix est pendu
    De cuer desirant
    Qu'on le voist ostant
    Et te[57] soit rendus.

64. Gens plains de meschance
    Viennent a puissance
    La ou Jhesus pend
    L'un prent une lance
    Ou coste lui lance
    Si qu'il l'euvre et fend.

65. Quant sa lance ostoit
    Du[58] coste yssoit[59]
    Sang en habondance
    Marie le voit
    Qui dueil en avoit
    Creez sans doubtance.

66. Longin fut cellui
    Qui ce cop fery
    Et ne veoit goutte
    Du sang qu'espandy
    Sur sa main chey[60]
    Puet estre une goutte.

67. Ses yeulx en frotta
    Dont prestement a
    Recouvré sa vue
    Dont que recevra[61]
    Cellui qui aura
    Sa loy soustenue.

68. Paine toy, labeure
    Jour, nuit, a toute heure.
    Entre en son coste
    S'en luy fais demeure
    Dy et si t'asseure
    Qu'as repos trouvé.[62]

69. Regarde comment
    Joseph et sa gent
    Et Nycodemus
    Compassiblement
    Et piteusement
    Regardent Jhesus.

70. Ilz vont saluer
    Et reconforter
    La tres glorieuse
    Et puis descloer
    Jhesus et oster
    De la croix honteuse.

71. Celle Vierge douce
    En moult grant angoisse
    Son Filz mort rechoit
    En son gron[63] le couche
    Les yeux[64] et la bouche
    Souvent lui baisoit.

A COMPLIE

72. Tres humainement
    Et devotement
    Le vouldrent laver
    Voluntairement
    En ton pensement
    Le pues essuer.

73. Espices et fleurs
    Et bonnes odeurs
    Ont mis entour lui
    Et en grans labeurs
    De plaintes et pleurs
    L'ont ensevely.[65]

74. Marie plouroit
    Quant de lui avoit
    La veue perdue
    Tousiours le voloit
    Voir s'elle povoit
    En sa face nue.

75. Tres reveramment
    Ce[66] corps excellent
    Au sepulchre portent
    Pa gemissement
    Au plourer forment
    L'un l'autre provocquent.

76. Quant la sont venu
    Marie a receu
    Son filz en ses bras
    Ceulx qui l'ont veu
    De pitie esmeu
    Peuent dire: Hellas.

77. Ces deux vrais amis
    Au sepulchre ont mis
    Nostre doulz sauveur
    Puis ont congie pris
    Et se sont assis
    En moult grant doleur.

78. Dueil mulitpliant
    Est en Marie quant[67]
    En[68] celle maniere
    Voit son doulz enfant
    Lequel amoit tant
    Demourer derriere.

79. Cy finent des diz
    Extrais et hors pris
    De la grief souffrance
    Du glorieux filz
    De Dieu en qui mis[69]
    Soit nostre esperance.

80. Prions a cellui
    Qui pour nous souffry
    Mort et passion
    Au grant Vendredy
    Que nos cuers en lui
    Tiengne en union. Amen

THE PASSION OF OUR LORD

1. To avoid evil, and bend thy thoughts unto the good: meditate upon these matters which I have long wished to relate in clear light.

2. Here then is the true reading of the Passion. It is good to be united to our Lord in his great sufferings.

AT MATINS

3. Go to the guest chamber; there thou shalt find thy Lord sitting down to meat, and from this place, meditate upon his deeds and words.

4. See, O sinner, how thy Lord humbled himself: with a meek heart and like a servant, he washeth his disciples's feet.

5. His body together with his blood, he did bless and consecrate, thus instituting his holy sacrament for our salvation.

6. In this holy sacrifice did he consecrate bread and wine for our great benefit, and did teach us the exalted and divine ministry of these.

7. Then, after supper, he led his disciples to the garden and, as they went, told them of the suffering which would come to him.

8. He taught them and exhorted them to prayer; then went he yonder and took with him John and James and Peter.

9. Then saith he unto them: "Pray that ye enter not into temptation." Then alone went he away and prayed.

10. Twice came he again unto his three friends lying there. He startled them and rebuked them for that they were sleeping.

11. He weighed in his heart and made his own his great Passion; and his body sweated blood that ran down to his feet.

12. Consider well how humbly and reverently the angel comforteth Jesus; how graciously he assisteth and strengtheneth him.

13. Then Jesus wipeth off sweat and blood from his face then cometh he to his three chosen friends and findeth them sleeping.

14. He wakened them and told them he was presently to be seized. Neither ran he away, but rather to the traitors did he surrender himself.

15. Judas the miscreant drew near unto Jesus and kisseth him. Thus displaying very great treachery, he kisseth him.

16. All are faint-hearted; there is none so bold as would dare touch him. Doubt not that Judas wondered thereon.

17. "Tell me, whom seek ye?" inquired our refuge. "It is he of Nazareth". Jesus then came forth and said: "I am he".

18. When they heard his voice, these villains fell to the ground in a faint. Twice thus did the gentle king of kings raise them again.

19. The Jews were sore afraid. Peter took heart again and drew his sword boldly and struck off the servant's ear.

20. Jesus took the ear and did replace it and heal him. Then they bound Jesus and took him away. O God, what a prize for those so bedevilled.

21. They seized Jesus and bound him and surrounded him jeering one and all. They led him away to the house of Annas, grievously tormenting him the while.

22. Many a bad kerl slapped him and insulted him greatly, then they led him away, beating and abusing him.

23. Likewise Annas sent his Lord, whom Judas had betrayed, bound and fettered, to the high priest Caiaphas who found no joy in it.

24. When he saw Jesus, he sat in the seat of judgement and questioned him. When Jesus heard him he told him the truth without ado.

25. Then could you see the wrathful Jews make great fuss and shout: "He is worthy of death".

26. These froward and insane people bespattered his face with foul and sinful spittle.

AT LAUDS

27. The miserable villains sat Jesus down and blindfolded him, then five or six of them smote him all around.

28. Saying without pretence: "Prophesy unto us, who is he that struck thee?" They held him, mocking and reviling him in various guise.

29. They pull out the beard of the all-loving one; they revile him; insult him; put him to shame.

30. Herein was fulfilled that which thou spakest the evening before: thy friends will be offended during the night.

31. They all fled away as though dazed. Thou art now alone among those rabbis like sheep among wolves.

AT PRIME

32. Now when morning was come, they led the Divine King to Pilate that he might put him to death, and they began to accuse him.

33. They brought forth false witnesses to accuse him, but the truly innocent one answered them naught.

34. Then, hustling and smiting him, they led Jesus unto Herod who came forward and accosted him.

35. He questioned him in many words, and inquired what he wished to know, but Jesus answered him not.

36. When Herod saw that he answered not, he nodded his head. He set him at nought, and deemed him a fool.

37. They arrayed him in a white garment so as to deride him. Thus were fools arrayed in these days.

38. Making merry with him, they led Jesus to Pilate. See the wondrous gift, how the all-bountiful purchaseth our love.

AT TERCE

39. See how Jesus is stripped naked by these deceitful brutes. Naked they bind him tightly to a post.

40. They smite and buffet him pitilessly with cruel whips and most wickedly wound and lacerate his precious body.

41. Seeing his pitiful estate, let not thy mind wander, yet look below and thou shalt see the earth steeped in his blood.

42. For bragging or revelry, they arrayed him in a scarlet robe and they put a reed in his hand for a sceptre.

43. Behold them crown thy God with cruel thorns: all this painful anguish willingly endured to redeem thee.

44. The Jews kneeled down before him and began to salute him; they smote him on his head and lacerated and struck him, and his blood did flow.

45. Pilate brought him out to them, hoping to assuage them with the sight of his piteous state, but the wicked mob cried out saying: "Crucify him!"

AT SEXT

46. Meditate in thine heart the harsh, cruel and unjust sentence passed on thy just and true God, the all-merciful.

47. They stripped him and gave him back his garments: they gave him great pain but methinks they felt nought of it.

48. Crowned and lacerated and bearing his cross, our paragon, hustled and buffeted, goeth up to Calvary.

49. Thou art so weak that thou canst not carry thy cross and on the way thou seest thy mother endure such sorrow.

50. When they were stripping him of his garments, his worthy wounds were opened and his blood flowed from his whole body. Let everyone hold this truth in memory.

51. The broken-hearted woman pushed and hove and jostled so, that with her kerchief she covered and hid his manhood.

52. See Jesus hanging on the cross, his arms and legs stretched out, his hands and feet pierced with nails.

AT NONE

53. They raise him between two robbers, the more to disparage him. This let us always meditate in our hearts if we be devout.

54. The weight of his body enlarged the holes in his hands and feet. Blood flowed therefrom and dropped to the ground and stained Mount Calvary.

55. Wicked and iniquitous are the villains who disown so piteous a God who prayeth for them that crucify him.

56. He thirsted for humanity's sake, but these felonious Jews gave him a very bitter draught.

57. Alas, ponder upon the wretched suffering and agony of God thy brother who commendeth his soul to God the Father.

58. In great agony he crieth out with a loud voice and giveth up the ghost which forthwith descendeth into hell and breaketh the gates asunder.

59. There he found the saints he did love of a perfect love. He consoled them and remained there until the third day.

AT VESPERS

60. When Jesus died, the sun was eclipsed and the rocks were rent and the earth did quake. And all feared exceedingly.

61. Saint Denis away in foreign parts foretold many of these happenings after which, through good judgement, he was baptised.

62. O Virgin Mary, grieving at the foot of the cross, thou art bedewed with the blood of the gentle fruit of life, the king of kings.

63. Thou weepest with fondness on thy dear child hanging on the cross, fervently desiring that he be taken down and returned to thee.

64. Men full of malice come in great force to the place where Jesus is hanging. One with a spear pierced his side, opening it and gashing it.

65. When the spear was withdrawn, his side did bleed exceedingly. Believe indeed that Mary witnessed this with great sorrow.

66. Longinus it was who speared Jesus's side. He saw not the blood he shed. On his hand, perchance, a drop did fall.

67. He rubbed his eyes and forthwith recovered his sight. Such a gift will he receive who keeps God's law.

68. Take pains and exert thyself, by day and by night and at all times. Make thine abode in his side, thus shalt thou be assured of finding rest.

69. See how Joseph and his retainers and Nicodemus behold Jesus with compassion and with sorrow.

70. They greet and comfort the most glorious virgin then they remove the nails and take down the body from the shameful cross.

71. The gentle virgin received with much grief her dead son and lay him in her lap. Again and again she kissed his eyes and mouth.

AT COMPLINE

72. They desired to wash him most gently and piously. Thou canst in thy thoughts wipe his body dry.

73. They bound the body with fragrant spices and flowers and with sorrowful sighs and pitiful mourning they shrouded him.

74. Mary wept when she could see him no more, for evermore she hoped to see his face again.

75. With great reverence, they carry to the tomb the glorious body, keening and wailing greatly.

76. And when they came there, Mary received her son in her arms and those who saw her were moved by pity. "Alas!" they sighed.

77. His two trusty friends laid our gentle saviour in the tomb, then, sitting over against the sepulchre and lamenting greatly, they departed thence.

78. Ever greater sorrow overcometh Mary as she beholdeth her gentle son whom she so loved.

79. Thus endeth the tale taken from the grievous Passion of the glorious son of God. Let us place our trust in him.

80. Let us pray to him who suffered and died on that Good Friday. May our hearts remain united in him. Amen.

PART II

CRITICAL COMMENTARY

DESCRIPTION AND HISTORY OF THE MANUSCRIPTS

The poem called "Heures de la Passion" has come down to us in three manuscripts: two of them are in France and one in the United States. All three manuscripts are in a superb condition of preservation, and two of them are illustrated.

They are:

PARIS - Bibliothèque Nationale Fonds français 190
CHANTILLY - Musée Condé 141
BOSTON (Mass.) - Public Library 1551 (= med.129)

PARIS - Bibliothèque Nationale Fonds Français 190

This is a fine manuscript with a long and interesting history. It first belonged to Louis of Bruges, who held the Lordship of the Gruythuyse[1] He was also Prince of Steenhuyse and Lord of Avelghem, Hamste, Oostcamp, Reveren, Thielt-ten-Hove and Espierres, Earl of Winchester and a Knight of the Order of the Golden Fleece. He was born in 1422. He came from a long line of distinguished warriors whose destinies were linked to those of the House of Burgundy and later to those of France. In 1449 he was cup-bearer to the Duke of Burgundy. Well-aware of his influence and popularity in Holland, Flanders and particularly in Bruges, the successive heads of the House of Burgundy used him repeatedly as an ambassador of goodwill in their various conflicts with the Northern Provinces. He also served the Dukes of Burgundy in their numerous affrays with other European Kings and

Princes. In 1455 he married Marguerite de Borsele, by whom he had several sons and daughters; he died on November 24, 1492.

A pious and erudite man, he loved the arts and possessed a superb library, rivalled only by that of the Dukes of Burgundy. He constantly added to his library through purchases and through his numerous commissions to scholars, poets, translators, painters and binders. A great number of his books were manufactured in Bruges and in nearby Ghent. He spared nothing in his efforts to enrich and beautify his library: the most renowned scribes and illustrators were called upon; the finest vellum used. The bindings were superb and were usually in fine velvets of various colours enhanced with corners and clasps of copper and silver gilt. On a great number of his manuscripts he had his heraldic bearings painted to which was added this motto in Flemish: *Meer es in tu*, sometimes given in French: *Plus est en vous*. At his death his eldest son, Jean, inherited the library. But in 1500, the fortunes of the Bruges family changed. For some obscure reason, the family fell foul of the King of England Henry VIII, and of Louis XII. Their name and immense possessions were soon no more. Among the despoliations they had to suffer was the seizure of their famous library which was annexed by Louis XII who incorporated it into his own in his residence at Blois. In so doing, the King had all of Louis de Bruges' arms and bearings erased, spunged off, or painted over with his own. In one case - a Latin text of Ptolemy's Geography - Louis XII was even conceited enough to have his own head painted over that of the previous owner. In 1544, the Blois library was transferred to Fontainebleau by Francis I and there it was inventoried, indicating, for each book, not only the author, content, binding and decoration, but also the place it had occupied at Blois. Then, together with the books that had belonged to Louis XI, Charles VIII, and Louis XII, they helped constitute the Bibliothèque du Roi and, much later, the Bibliothèque Nationale.[2]

Manuscript 190 of the Paris Bibliothèque Nationale (ancien fonds) was part of the library of Louis de Bruges. It bore the recension number 312. It then appears in the Bibliothèque du Roi under the number 6850 and is now shelved as: ancien fonds français 191.[3] The book used to be bound in velvet[4] but was rebound in red morocco and is stamped with the arms of

France on front- and off-boards. It is a large in-folio-maximo volume containing 348 folios of which three are left blank and seven are devoted to the table of contents.

It is written on vellum in very large old bastard hand and P. Paris[5] is of the opinion that the writing is that of Louis de Bruges' scribe who, between 1480 and 1483, manufactured another seven volumes. It is written on 2 columns throughout of 28 lines each.

The manuscript is decorated with five historiated letters, each introducing a section of text. The last section has none. They represented the arms and motto of Louis de Bruges. The arms have been painted over with those of France and in many cases so have the occurrences of the motto. P. Paris thinks that the miniatures were painted in Bruges.[6]

The manuscript contains the following items:

1r. – 63v.	Le secret parlement de l'homme contemplatif a son ame...[7]
64r. – 103r.	Le livre de contemplation[7]
103v. – 183r.	Devotions ordonnez par Frere Bonaventure[8]
183v. – 207r.	Le livre des quatre vertus traduit de Seneque par Jehan Trousseau[9]
207v. – 237r.	Moralites de philosophie[10]
237v. – end	Regles pour bien entendre la messe.

Our text is to be found among the 38 devotional pieces translated or imitated from St. Bonaventure. It is the fourteenth piece and is found on fols. 129 - 134, entitled: "Heures de la Passion de Jhesus-Crist par vers et bons metres de six". The indications of Canonical Hours are given in the margin in extremely fine script, in a 17th century hand.[11]

CHANTILLY - Musée Condé 141 (1474)

Compared with that of the Bibliothèque Nationale manuscript, the history of the Chantilly manuscript is virtually unknown.

It previously bore the marks   XIV^F 1474
                                          17   Po

It is bound in green morocco with gilt edges and measures 190 x 135 mm. It is written on vellum and has 36 folios, of which one is left blank at the beginning, and two at the end of the volume. It has no miniatures, but the initials are slightly decorated. In the "Passion" the first initial: P, is illuminated. It is larger and extends onto four lines. The workmanship is very simple: a few spirals inside the loop of the letter and three skimpy sprays of three-petalled flowers painted in two colours and placed at the three available corners of the frame for the letter. The initial letter at the beginning of each verse has been hastily enclosed in a penned frame: scallops or parallel lines with a few tendrils here and there. Quite unaccountably, some initials are preceded by pen flourishes in the shape of waves.

    The text is written in full-line, 14 lines to the page in two different hands. It is rubricated.

    The contents of the manuscript are divided into two equal parts, each corresponding to a different scribal hand. The first part (folios 1 - 16v.) is a collection of devotional poems and prayers:

1r. - 3v.	C'est salutation de l'ange Gabriel pour nostre redemption: je te salue Maria[12]
3v. - 4v.	Une devote oroison de nostre dame: Douce Vierge Marie....
4v. - 9r.	Devote salutation : Dame je vous rend le salut....[13]
9r. - 11r.	Une tres devote devote (*sic*) recommendation a la vierge Marie: O tres glorieuse tres haulte....
11v. - 16v.	Obsecro en franloy (*sic*) bien devote: Je te prie ma dame saincte Marie....

The second part (fols. 17r.–33v.) contains the Hours of the Passion, without incipit. This part also exhibits two inscriptions, in a contemporary hand: at the bottom of fol. 17r. in cursive hand:

    "esperance me soutien et souvenir me tue"

and at the top of fol. 34v. in bastard hand:
"secret et discret".

BOSTON (Mass.) - Public Library 1551 (= Med. 129)

The early history of this manuscript is unknown. It came up for sale by Maggs Bros. Ltd., London, in 1953 and appeared in the centenary catalogue of that firm (No. 812) as item No. 17. All efforts made to obtain information from Maggs regarding the early history of the manuscript have been in vain. The Boston Public Library purchased the manuscript on 1st April, 1954. The asking price was £225 and the purchaser paid $585. The manuscript was bought with the help of the Josiah H. Benton fund and it received the accession number 033. A recent hand has added '1470' on the first folio.

Josiah H. Benton (1843 - 1917) was of English descent and his family had settled in Connecticut in 1630. He was a lawyer and practised in Lancaster. He was involved in politics and, in 1869, became private secretary to the governor of New Hampshire.

His biographer[14] indicated that he settled in Boston in 1872 "and was actively identified from that time with the development of the city." He adds:

> "In 1894 he became a member of the board of trustees of the Boston Public Library, giving conspicuous service as president of the board during the last nine years of his life. From 1909 to 1913 he was chairman of the board of trustees of the Massachusetts State Library. From 1910 to 1917 he was a trustee of Boston University. Throughout his life he collected editions of the English Prayer Book and related material to show its origin and growth. At his death this unique and valuable collection of six hundred and twenty-one items was bequeathed to the Boston Public Library."

Benton left a substantial legacy to the Boston Public Library for the further acquisition of books and manuscripts.

The book is bound in claret-coloured morocco. It is blind-stamped on the front- and off-boards with a design of Christ in Majesty in a frame of grapevines and two medallions of an unidentified old man. The inside board displays a gold *dentelle* on its borders and it is stamped 'Ch. de Samblanx 1921'.

Charles de Samblanx was a binder in Paris and he is mentioned in Y. Devaux's *Dix siècles de reliure*. He was born in Brussels in 1855 and died in Paris in 1943.[15]

The manuscript, which is written and decorated on very fine and smooth cream coloured vellum measures 200 x 400 mm. It has 23 folios.

It is decorated with seven miniatures (and not eight as stated in Maggs' Catalogue) painted in *grisaille* with very faint traces of gold and a few colours. These are placed at the beginning of each Canonical Hour and measure 76/78 x 60 mm.

They are:

The betrayal in the garden of Gethsemane	:	Matins
Jesus before Pilate	:	Prime
The scourging of Jesus	:	Terce
Jesus carrying his cross	:	Sext
Jesus dies on the cross	:	None
The descent from the cross	:	Vespers
The entombment	:	Compline

The first folio displays a floral border painted without background, directly onto the vellum, in gold and colours. The initials following each miniature are decorated. The other initials are only slightly enlarged and less decorated. The decoration of the manuscript is described and discussed at length in Chapter 6.

The writing corresponds to what J. Stiennon[16] describes as "lettre de forme des ducs de Bourgogne." and what N. de Wallis[17] describes more generally as "écriture mixte gothique". The initials at the beginning of each line are in semi-gothic. This writing presents similarities with the writing of Jean Duquesne, who was a scribe of Louis de Bruges, but certain elements make it quite clear that he cannot have written this manuscript. On the other hand it has two features in common with the writing of David Aubert: the S's and f's which are done with one instead of two strokes (as is always the case for Duquesne), and also the very fine curlicues above the downward hafts of most letters, especially *t*, *e* and *s* (in end position). This writing can be found in Ms. 456 of the Dutuit Collection: *Histoire du bon Roi Alexandre* in the "cinquiesme voeu du paon a la cour du roi Porus." Delaissé left a handwritten note on a facsimile of this in the Courtauld Institue, London, stating that it was in the Burgundian Library already in 1467. The scribe was possibly David Aubert. This scribe's handiwork can also be seen in the superb volumes of the Chronicle of the Counts of Flanders in the Holkham Hall Library (Ms 659). The Chronicle was illustrated by the Master of Mary of Burgundy in 1477 and written by David Aubert who was born at Hesdin and was writing in Brussels around 1460. He then moved to Bruges aroung the year 1467 before working at Ghent in 1474.

Our manuscript contains only the *Passion* poem in 80 stanzas, (plus 2)[18] and not 83, as stated by Maggs.

NOTES

1. *Gruythuyse* (also *Gruthuyse, Gruthuse, Gruuthuuse*), a Flemish expression meaning: The House of the *Gruyte*. The gruyte was a taxation on the production and sale of beer payable to this House. As to their motto which in modern Flemish would read: *Meer is in 't U*, it means: *There is more in you* (i. e.: more than you think).

2. For further information on Louis de Bruges and his library, see *Bibliographie nationale de Belgique*, Bruxelles, 1881-3. cols. 381 - 390 (with further bibliography) and O. van Praet, *Recherches sur Louis de Bruges*, Paris, 1831.

3. In the Pauline recension it bears the number 197 (see P. Paris *Les manuscrits français de la bibliothèque du Roi*, Paris, 1838, Tome II, pp. 115-128).

4. See O. van Praet, *op. cit.*, p. 114.

5. See P. Paris, *op. cit.*, p. 127.

6. *Loc. cit.*

7. De Jean Gerson.

8. "Recueil de trente-huit pièces dévotes traduites ou imitées de St. Bonaventure" in *Bibliothèque nationale - Catalogue des manuscrits français: Anciens fonds*. Tome I Paris, 1868.

9. The *explicit* indicates that Jehan Trousseau made this translation in Bourges (Berry) in 1372.

10. It would seem that the author is also Jehan Trousseau.

11. It should be noted that the indications of Canonical Hours appear at the same places in the poem in all three manuscripts; in the Boston version the words are replaced by appropriate miniatures.

12. On two rhymes: *a* and *e*.

13. All in feminine rhymes.

14. See *Dictionary of American Biography* under "Benton, Josiah Henry."

15. Y. Devaux, *Dix siècles de reliure*, Paris (Pygmalion), 1977, p. 380.

16. J. Stiennon, *Paléographie du Moyen Age*, Paris,(Colin),1966, see p. 121.

17. N. de Wallis, *Eléments de paléographie*, Paris, 1838.

18. About the two additional stanzas, see Appendix A.

PRINCIPLES AND METHOD OF EDITING

The principal aim of this chapter is to discover which, if any, of the three manuscripts that contain the *Passion* text is the original (author's copy); or, failing that, to identify the ancestor of the manuscripts available. This can be either an extant manuscript, or a lost one whose existence can be postulated through the application of the method described below. For this purpose I use the method I have previously adopted in editing texts.[1] It is based closely upon that devised by the late Dom Froger of Solesmes.[2]

Principles

The following principles have to be kept in mind:[3]

1. When copying a text, independent scribes may make mistakes in different places.

2. Generally, each scribe reproduces the mistakes of his model to which he adds his own mistakes.

3. Hence, a scribal error is usually transmitted to all the manuscripts copied on the faulty model, thus defining its lineage: it is a faulty group (see below, note 4). The groups belonging to one lineage get smaller as they become further removed from the original, since each descendant contains one manuscript less.

4. It is evident that different mistakes contribute to the creation of different affiliations or collateral groups. These groups differ completely and have no manuscript in common.

5. Lastly, if one group ramifies, its descendants are necessarily fragmentations of it.

Thus, normally, groups do not overlap. Yet it may happen that two or more scribes correct an obviously faulty text in the same manner. This produces an apparent contamination (the two scribes may have lived in places widely apart or even at different times). The editor has to be extremely cautious regarding isolated "contaminations."

Method

In order to reconstruct the genealogical tree, three steps have to be followed:

1. *Adopt arbitrarily a reference manuscript* with which all the others will be compared and list all variants from this reference manuscript.

2. *Group these variants*, thus establishing their relationship to the reference manuscript. The latter is, *for the time being*, arbitrarily considered as the ancestor. For this reason, the stemma is so far only fictitiously oriented. None the less, manuscripts bear a real relationship with each other.

3. *Give the stemma its true orientation*, by diagrammatically relating all the manuscripts to the true ancestor (i.e. the manuscript, either extant or lost, which contains no mistakes). To accomplish this, the variants are no longer considered vis-à-vis the reference manuscript, but as mistakes in the absolute sense. In cases where the reference manuscript (= the fictitious ancestor) chosen proves to be the true ancestor, then the fictitious orientation coincides with the true orientation.

The ancestor being the manuscript which contains none of the mistakes discovered through the collation of variants, we are left with two possibilities:

1. either the ancestor has no mistakes at all, in which case it is the original manuscript (the author's copy);

2. or, it is a faulty copy of the original and its mistakes appear in all manuscripts, unless these have been corrected, conjecturally or otherwise, by subsequent scribes.

It is impossible to go back further into the genealogy of the manuscripts. It goes without saying that any corrections made by modern editors for any reason whatever should be plainly advertised as such.

Application

The three manuscripts in which the text of the *Passion* has come down to us, we designate as follows:

  Boston Public Library   = B
  Chantilly Musée Condé   = C
  Bibliothèque Nationale Paris   = N

I have chosen the Boston manuscript (= B) as reference copy, as it was easier of access to me and could be consulted directly (without recourse to microfilms).

The list of variants as appearing in the *apparatus criticus* (at the end of this chapter) enables us to group the manuscripts in the following manner:

BN *versus* C:	2-4-23-38-54-68	= 6
CN *versus* B:	1-3-5-7-9-14-16 18-40-41-44-45-46- 47-53-64-67-69	= 18
BC *versus* N:	6-8-10-11-12-13- 19-20-21-22-25-26- 27-28-29-30-31-32- 33-34-36-37-39-42- 48-49-50-51-52-55- 56-57-58-59-60-61- 62-65-66	= 39
B *versus* C *versus* N:	15-17-24-35-43-63	= 6

Thus B having been arbitrarily chosen as reference manuscript, the variant groups appear as follows:

    Group C [4] :   frequency 6
    Group CN :   frequency 18
    Group N   :   frequency 39

The six cases where the three manuscripts differ are, of course, of no use for the establishment of the stemma.

We next have to establish the relationships of the variant groups. This may be represented diagrammatically. First comes the large group consisting of all the manuscripts, that is, when all manuscripts agree. Then, underneath this, are written all the other variant groups in decreasing order of importance (degree of variance). In each group I have shaded the manuscripts which, placed underneath it, are its descendants in the orientation arbitrarily adopted: in this way a group completely shaded represents a manuscript now lost, but which may be presumed to have existed in the past. Lost manuscripts are designated by a small letter (x, y, z...) to distinguish them from extant manuscripts represented by capital letters.

Thus we have:

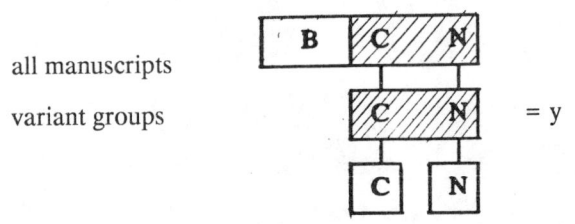

all manuscripts

variant groups   = y

Next we may transcribe this information in the shape of a stemma:

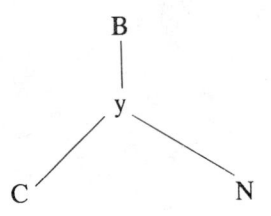

This stemma gives a true picture of the inter-relationship of the several manuscripts but, since B was chosen arbitrarily as ancestor, the *orientation* is fictitious.

In order to give the stemma its real orientation, however, we have to apply the notion of error, i. e. we have to study which groups are faulty. Turning back once again to the *apparatus criticus* (and the text itself) we find that the fautly groups are distributed in the following nammer.

		No. of faults
BN		(= 0)
CN	1 - 16 - 46 - 47 - 53	(= 5)
BC		(= 0)
C	4 - 68	(= 2)
B	5 - 7 - 9 -18 - 44 - 45 - 69	(= 7)
N	6 - 10 - 11 - 12 - 13 - 22 - 25 - 26 - 27 - 28 - 29 - 31 - 33 - 34 - 42 - 55 - 57 - 58 - 62 - 65	(= 20)

If we now circle the faulty groups we obtain the following:

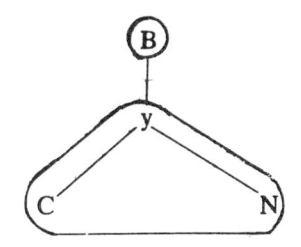

The now lost manuscript *y* must be included in the same faulty group as C and N since it displays necessarily all the readings of CN including the errors which made up the CN group for, whatever the orientation, it is an intermediary between C and N.

From this arrangement our conclusions clearly emerge, namely, all the manuscripts in this stemma are faulty and none of them is the ancestor. The pure text (ancestor) can only be placed on the stemma at a point free from errors, i.e at some point on the line from B to y.

In its true orientation, the stemma now becomes;

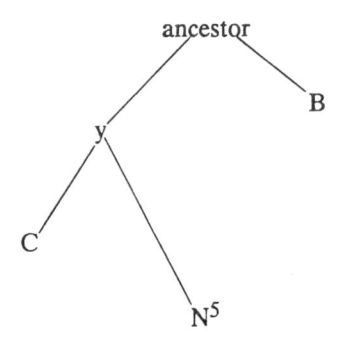

Restitution of the text

According to this stemma, the reading of the ancestor is given:
- a. when y and B agree (i. e. when CBN agree; all the manuscripts extant)
- b. when B and C agree against N: errors in N
- c. when B and N agree against C: errors in C

The restitution is undecided when we have CN against B. It is then left to us to make a decision based on grammatical and stylistic correction, context and other factors.

There are 18 cases where CN and B disagree. But since there are 5 cases (readings 1 - 16- 46 - 47 - 53) where CN is in error and 7 cases (reading 5 - 7 - 9 - 18 - 44 - 45 - 69) where B is in error, we can account for 12 out of the 18 cases. The remaining 6 cases (3 - 14 - 40 - 41 - 64 - 67) are, I think, equally acceptable. In view of its closeness to the ancestor, I have in each case chosen the reading of B as being generally more in keeping with the grammar, the style, the count of syllables and general trend of the surpreme ancestor.

In establishing the *apparatus criticus*, I have ignored the graphical differences which are common in texts of that period, either because they are the same letter (u, n for instance) or because they are, either singly or in group, employed indifferently (v, u; i, u; s, x, z; sc sct, *etc*...). The Boston manuscript is the only one to differentiate clearly between u and n and between c and t.

No punctuation is given in any of the three manuscripts. I have supplied a minimum of punctuation for the sake of clarity of understanding.

Lastly, the *apparatus criticus* is positive and thoroughly repertoried; that is, each reading has been assigned a number (1 to 69) which is kept for all textual references; this is followed by the reference in the text: stanza number (1 through 80) followed by line number (1 through 6). Then follow the readings: the first one being that adopted in the text, the second (and eventually third) being the others. Thus reading 33 can be found in stanza 31, line 5. B and C have the adopted reading: "comme les brebis", whereas N's reading; "comme la doulce brebiz" has not been adopted.

Apparatus criticus

1. 2.3 B) Des principaulx / CN) Les principaulx
2. 4.4-5 BN) De tant humble cuer comme serviteur /C) comme serviteur de tant humble cuer
3. 7.5 B) qu'a luy / CN) qui luy
4. 8.1-6 BN) cp. whole stanza 3rd pers. sing/ C) Tu les...Tu les...puis d'eux t'eslongnas...Et a toy menas
5. 9.1 CN) orez / B) oyez
6. 9.6 BC) en devotion / N) en sa devotion
7. 10.1 CN) s'est / B) est
8. 10.5 BC) et tres / N) et moult
9. 11.1 CN) cuer / B) corps
10. 13.1 BC) oste / N) ostez
11. 13.1 BC) Jhesus / N) a Jhesus
12. 13.3 BC) qu'ot sue / N) qu'il sue
13. 13.6 BC) qu'a dormant trouvé / N) que dormant a trouvé
14. 14.3 B) vint / CN) vient
15. 14.4 B) se mua / C) se muca / N) s'en mua
16. 14.6 B) aux felons soy rendre / CN) Aux faulx felons rendre
17. 15.2 B) va / C) vient / N) vint
18. 16.1 CN) tous / B) tout
19. 16.2 BC) eut si / N) ot tant
20. 16.3 BC) fust sy / N) fust tant
21. 16.4 BC) de toucher / N) d'attoucher
22. 20.4 BC) se fait / N) fut faitte
23. 20.4 BN) la / C) sa
24. 22.5 B) batus et chassiez / C) boutés et gectés / N) bouté et chacié
25. 23.4 BC) qu'ot livré Judas / N) qu'il livre a Judas
26. 23.5 BC) au grant / N) et au grant
27. 23.6 BC) qui n'en eut / N) qui en orent
28. 24.2 BC) ou siege s'assist / N) Pylate se assist
29. 28.3 BC) qui cy / N) qui t'a ores
30. 31.1 BC) s'en sont fuiz / N) s'en sont ja fuiz

31.	31.3	BC) et tu ez tout / N) et tu restes tous
32.	31.4	BC) ces / N) iceulz
33.	31.5	BC) comme les brebis / N) comme la doulce brebiz
34.	31.6	BC) sont entre les leups / N) qui est entre les leuz
35.	32.5	B) que le mette a fin / C) qui le mette a fin / N) qu'il le mette a fin
36.	33.3	BC) cy accusé ont / N) accusé ilz ont
37.	34.2	BC) sacquant et boutant / N) sacquantet hurtant
38.	35.6	BN) un mot / C) nul mot
39.	36.3	BC) rescout / N) tourna
40.	37.1	B) desguisement / CN) desguiseement
41.	37.3	B) revestir lui / CN) vestir ilz lui
42.	37.4	BC) que fole / N) la fole
43.	38.2	B) mené ont / C) mene on / N) remaine on
44.	38.6	CN) achate / B) embrace
45.	39.6	CN) l'ont / B) ont
46.	45.5	B) crie / CN) crient
47.	49.3	B) jusqu'au / CN) jusques au
48.	49.6	BC) endurer / N) demener
49.	50.1	BC) on / N) l'on
50.	50.1	BC) desvestoit / N) despouilloit
51.	54.4	BC) yssoit / N) partoit
52.	54.6	BC) mont / N) monde
53.	55.1	B) parceux / CN) preceux
54.	56.2	BN) tres grans / C) tres haulx
55.	61.1	BC) de ce saint / N) de ce fait saint
56.	62.1	BC) O Vierge / N) Ha Vierge
57.	63.6	BC) et te / N) et qu'il te
58.	65.2	BC) du / N) de ce
59.	65.2	BC) yssoit / N) sailloit
60.	66.5	BC) main chey / N) main en chey
61.	67.4	BC) dont que / N) mais que
62.	68.6	BC) qu'as repos / N) qu'as bon repos
63.	71.4	C) gron / B) giron / N) geron

64.	71.5	B)	yeux et / CN) mains et
65.	73.6	BC)	l'ont ensevely / N) l'ont bien ensevely
66.	75.2	BC)	ce / N) le
67.	78.2	B)	est en Marie quant / CN) en Marie est quant
68.	78.3	BN)	en celle / C) Qu'en celle
69.	79.5	CN)	mis / B) pris

NOTES

1. See N. Marzac, *Richard Rolle de Hampole*[...]Paris (Librairie Philosophique Vrin) 1968. pp. 69 ff. and *Robert Ciboule: Edition critique du sermon "Qui manducat me"*[...]Cambridge (MHRA) 1971. Pp. 15 ff.

2. See J. Froger, *La critique des textes et son automatisation*. Paris, (Dunod), 1968, as well as numerous articles.

3. Translation and adaptation of these points from my edition of Ciboule's sermon, cited above, are made possible through the courtesy of MHRA, Cambridge.

4. The term "group", though often referring to several manuscripts, may also properly be applied to a single manuscript of a given lineage.

5. In this representation N is placed lower than C to indicate that it is much more faulty than C.

PROSODIC AND LINGUISTIC ASPECTS

A. Format of the text

In all three manuscripts, the "Hours of the Passion" are in the form of an 80-stanza poem. The text is consistent in all three cases: the stanzas are of 6 lines each and are in fact, as we shall see later, double tercets. Each line has 5 syllables throughout the poem. The rhyme pattern is absolutely constant: *a a b a a b*.

The pentasyllabic line, used as an important element within the structure of a poem, is rare. Henri Chatelain remarks: [1]

> "Depuis Agnès de Navarre jusqu'à Chartier il apparait dans quelques strophes longues [...]. Martial d' Auvergne, les fatistes et les rhétoriqueurs l'emploient aussi aux mêmes usages [...] mais aussi a des couplets plus courts, huitains, sixains, cinquains".

In fact, Chatelain has listed 5-syllable lines in XVth century poetry whose rhymes follow the repeated pattern *a a b* (in other words, the repeated tercet)[2] They can be found in Arnoul Greban's *Passion*; in *Le Mystère de Saint Laurent*; the *Mystère des trois Doms; La Vie et la Passion de Monseigneur Saint Didier* and *Le Mystère de Saint Quentin*.[3] In all, he collected 86 stanzas, of which it should be noted that only 24 follow the same rhyme pattern as ours, that is, the rhyme varies after each double tercet; while the other 62 follow rhymes of the type *a a b a a b / b b c b b c /* etc.

If then, the *a a b a a b* form is frequent,[4] it is far less so when linked to the pentasyllabic line and I have not found another poem completely composed in this form.

In what circumstances was the 5-syllable line used in the XVth century? E. Langlois in his *Recueil d'arts de seconde rhétorique* offers the opinions of several theoreticians.[5]

In his *Arts de rhétorique*, Molinet writes:

"Autre taille de vers sixains se font en moralitez et jeux de personnages, souverainement en reproches ou redargutions; et sont communement de six lignes, de cinq et de vj sillabes.

> *La guerre*
> J'ay bruit, regne et cours
> En champs et en cours
> En l'autre et en l'une.
>
> *La Paix*
> Je suis sans secours
> Mais apres decours
> Voit on prime lune".[6]

It should be noted here that the form is that of a double tercet rhyming *a a b a a b* . If this form be used for "redargutions" as is the case here, it is also used for "reproches" and we are immediately reminded of the *Improperia* which are part of the Good Friday Office, and this, of course, fits our case to perfection. Another text published by Langlois (his sixth) is an anonymous treatise entitled *Traité de rhétorique*. It dates from the end of the XVth century and originated in Picardy.[7] The author writes:

> RIMES DE V. PIEDZ ET SIX LIGNES. VERS SIXAINS.
> Vers qui sont sizains
> De .v. piedz attains
> Que les fect rimer
> De plours et de plains
> Et de mos bien plains
> Font les gens plourer.
>
> AULTRES VERS SIZAINS.
> Congiés et adieux,
> Regretz, plaintes, dieulx
> Et gemissement
> De pecheurs vers cieulx
> Que dorment es cieulz
> Se font bien souvent.[8]

Here again the author uses the rhyme pattern *a a b a a b*. As to the subjects that are pertinent to "vers sixains" (i.e. 6-line stanzas with 5 syllables to the line), we learn that they can express sorrow and lamentation and induce sadness. They are apt for rendering the sufferings of parting and of the sinful soul.

In the second tercet, the 5th line makes little sense and Langlois, who is not certain of his reading, suggests an alternative: *domine*. In any case, the purport attributed to "vers sixains" is quite clear.

Under his No. 25 (p.261), the author gives a lay composed of twelve pentasyllabic lines uniformally rhyming *a a b a a b*. It is a farewell to the town of St. Omer where he expresses his sorrow and distress.

Another anonymous author to whom we owe *L'art et science de rhétorique vulgaire* dating from 1524/5,[9] reproduces textually the definitions given earlier by Molinet, only changing *reproches* for *proces*. He offers the following example:

> *Noblesse dit*
> Guerre plus ne poingt,
> Dont France est en point
> Avecq paix heureuse.
>
> *Le commun*
> Le roy l'a appoint,
> Doncq ne fuyons point
> Amour desireuse.[10]

Here again, we have the same form of stanza and rhyme but the banality of the thought is all too evident. Further on, he gives examples of *rondeaux* made into *chansons* "de toutes quantitez de sillabes" (p.284). As for the pentasyllabic lines, he gives an 8-line monorhymed poem on the absence of a friend.

The interest of this last author does not, of course, reside in his originality, but rather in the fact that, until 1525 at least, the theories gathered by Molinet were still valid.

To sum up, if one refers to the Arts of Second Rhetoric (i.e. poetry) of the time, one learns that the form of the *Passion* poem studied here was the one considered appropriate for the expression of suffering and sadness, and could evoke separation from a beloved being, lamentations and regrets. It also calls to mind the *Improperia* of Good Friday: all these topics and sentiments are obviously in perfect harmony with the themes and episodes of the Passion of Christ.

B. Syllable Count

Technically, our text is relatively simple. Nowhere can one detect the "procédés, gymastique de mots, difficultés cherchées pour le plaisir de les vaincre" mentioned by Chatelain about mediaeval poetry.[11] With but few exceptions the text is easy to understand, the style is straightforward, and grammatical rules are respected. The same applies to the syllable count. The key remark about this aspect is made by George Lote. Speaking of the Middle French period, he writes: "On rime comme on parle, et telle est la loi générale".[12] Thus the "mètre imparfait" mentioned by Jean Molinet in *Arts de rhétorique* (that is, a line ending with a "feminine diction" which exceeds the perfect metre by one syllable) is plentiful in our text, as indeed it is in all late mediaeval poetry. A stanza from Greban's *Passion* has several examples of this:

> Ce noble exempla*ire*
> bon Dieu, vous decla*ire*
> aux humains enclins
> Les vueillans retra*ire*
> qui a grant contra*ire*
> vous tous a declin.

(1st day; *Seraphin* speaking, lines 3669 - 3674, ed. G. Paris). A stanza from our *Passion* presents the same characteristics:

> Ce saint sacri*fice*
> Par grant bene*fice*
> Sacra pain et vin
> Eulx estant prop*ice*
> En aprist l'of*fice*
> Tres hault et divin. (st. 6)

Although variety in the syllable count may thus result from the use of the 'feminine ending' this is not the only determining factor. The use of vocalic groups sounded as diphthongs serves as a further determinant, and we have now to examine the text for specific examples.

The most common combination is IE. I have collected 48 examples of this group, of which more than three quarters (38) are sounded as diphthongs and therefore count as single syllables. In the remaining 10 cases, however, the group IE is not sounded as a diphthong. The reason for these discrepancies is most probably to be found in the necessities of metre. Thus *baisier* (15.1) accounts for 2 syllables and *buffiez* (22.1) for 3 syllables; *veissiez* (25.1) accounts for 3 syllables and *traittiez* (48.4) for 2 syllables; *vie* (62.5) accounts for 1 syllable; *prie* (55.1) for 2 syllables and *Marie* (65.4) for 3 syllables. Similarly, *priere* (8.3) accounts for 2 syllables and *maniere* (78.3) also for 2 syllables, thus giving 2 different values to IE.

Certain combinations are always sounded as diphthongs: IEN: *bien* (12.1); IEU: *lieu* (20.2; 59.1); *Dieu* (20.5 etc.,); whereas others are never sounded as diphthongs: IEUX: *injurieux* (29.4); *precieux* (40.6); *glorieux* (79.4) etc.

In the vocalic combination EU, the distribution is more even. EU counts as one syllable in *esleus* (13.5); *eut* (16.2 and 23.6); *receu* (76.2) and *esmeu* (76.5). It counts for 2 syllables in *cheus* (18.3)[13] and *veu* (76.4). As to the word *veue* (74.3), the distribution of syllables is more complicated. The line reads:

la veue perdue

The word *veue* counts for 2 syllables in any case but it can be divided in either of two ways: as *ve - ue* or as *veu-e*.

For the combination OE, I have only found the example *cloer* which, in both instances in the text (52.6 and 70.4), counts as 2 syllables.

In the group OI, the endings of the imperfect (2nd person singular and 3rd person plural) are sounded as diphthongs. Thus *estoient* (10.3); *dormoient* (10.6); *pouvoies* (49.1); *estoies* (49.2). There is one exception: *portoient* (37.6) in the line

Portoient adont

Here *portoient* counts for 3 syllables, the syllable *ent* forming an hiatus with the *a* of *adont*. It has to be admitted that this is a poor line. In the words *oyr* (18.1) and *oyt* (24.4) the vowel *i* (y) is in hiatus and these words count as 2 syllables. As to the word *maleois* (18.2), an adjective formed on the past participle of *maleïr*, the *e* is in hiatus and the word is pronounced as 3 syllables.

The vocalic group UA does not diphthongize: *institua* (5.6); *mua* (14.4).

In the group UE, diphthonging does not occur if the *e* is accented (past participle; part of infinitive) *sué* (13.3); *saluer* (44.3). In all other cases diphthonging takes place: *cuer* (4.4. etc.); *pues* (43.1 etc..); *dueil* (65.5 etc..).

No well-defined rule seems to apply to the combination UI. It is generally treated as one syllable: *nuit* (68.2); *depuis* (3.4); *puis* (7.1); *luy* (7.5) etc..); *fruit* (62.5); *pluiseurs* (60.6) etc. The word *Juis* - also spelled *Juifs*, etc. - (19.1 etc.) never accounts for 2 syllables and we have, for instance, *deguisement* (37.2) which does not diphthongize, and *guise* (42.6) which does. Here again, I think that the irregularity must be attributed to the fact that the poet treated these vocalic groups as flexible elements for the syllable count.

Finally, here are a few vocalic groups which do not diphthongize: words ending in -ion: *passion* (2.2); *union* (2.5; 80.6); *temptacion* (9.3); *devotion* (9.6) etc. The same is true of *huans* (21.3); *Cayphas* (23.5); *creez* (65.6); *crueux* (40.3); *fouets* (40.3); *tousiours* (74.4).

In conclusion, it seems clear that the author treated his task anything but lightly. Not one of the 480 lines of the poem is metrically incorrect, even if he sometimes had to resort to contrivances such as counting *courchiez* (25.2) as 3 syllables and *courchie* (51.1) as 2 syllables. We also read (31.2): *Com tous esbahis* and (31.5) *Comme les brebis*. Yet, in the end, these devices are not numerous and prove, at least, that the poet made every effort to perfect the details of his text.

To sum up the findings, we can say that only group IEN always diphthongizes and groups OE, UA and ION never diphthongize. Group OI diphthongizes in verbal endings. Group IE diphthongizes in a proportion of 4 to 1 whereas EU presents an equal distribution and UI does not obey any definite rule.

C. Types and phonetics of rhymes

Among the theoreticians of the Arts of Second Rhetoric, it is the Anonyme Lorrain who, more than the others, theorises on the art of rhyming. For him: "Rimer n'est autre chose que faire deux bastons finer de telle lettre ainsy bien l'un que l'autre" and he adds: "et plus resambleront l'un l'autre en la fin, meilleur sera la rime".[14] He thus recommends rich rhymes. The types of rhymes are very numerous. Langlois's *index* gives at least twenty, but George Lote soberly sums up the position thus:

> "Les séries données par les différents *Arts de Seconde Rhétorique* n'ont qu'une valeur purement indicative, mais ne prétendent nullement fixer un bon usage contre lequel il serait interdit de s'insurger. Il n'existe d'ailleurs aucune autorité qui se mêle d'approuver ou de défendre: chacun agit comme bon lui semble sous sa propre responsabilité, en partant de ce principe général, mais pas toujours très rigoureusement observé, que les fins de vers doivent être homophones".

Further on, he adds: "Les maladroits, quand la rime vient à leur manquer, ont souvent recours à l'assonnace."[15]

As regards the *Passion*, one finds very few "rimes riches", that is, rhymes having at least two homophonous syllables. Jean Molinet gives examples of these and they are words constructed on the same root, for instance: poser / apposer / deposer / composer / reposer / proposer / supposer[16]; the author of the *Passion* avoids even facile rhymes using long substantival endings: *-alite*; *-ition*; or adverbial endings: *-remment*. In the *Passion* text I can find only two such rhymes: *ditter / meditteés* (st.1); *proprement / sacrement* (st. 5), and perhaps *ouverte / couverte* (st. 41).

The "rime léonine" is a more usual form, that is, a rhyme having one homophonous syllable. Thus we have: *yras / trouveras* (st. 3): *lez / alez* (st.9); *prophetisa / baptisa* (st. 61) etc.

The "rime suffisante", also called "sonnante" - consisting of the vowel and consonant - is the most usual type of rhyme in the *Passion* text. It is obviously the easiest and was sometimes called "rime commune" - and it would therefore be tedious to give random examples of this type of rhyme. But we must give credit to our author for avoiding fairly successfully the use of what we call to-day "rime pauvre", in fact an assonance, and which XVth-century poets called "rime d'un voieux", that is , a mere repetition of the tonic vowel; thus the Anonyme Lorrain writes:[17]

>Exemple de rimer d'un voieux:
>Amor son prosme tout ainsy
>Comme ans ameroit son amy.

Thus we find *assis / ditz* (st. 3); *sacra / institua* (st. 5); *mua / va* (st. 14) etc.

Some rhymes in the text give us an interesting insight into XVth century pronunciation. Although the occasional "rime pour l'oeil" cannot be dismissed, I consider that 11 rhymes deserve attention.

St.1. The adjective *cler* rhymes with three infinitives: *eviter*; *excerciter*; *ditter*. Both Chatelain[18] and Langlois's *Recueil* attest that *r* is pronounced at the end of a word, and one finds in Choinet's *Livre des trois eages*,[19] *escorcher* rhyming with *chair* (9v. 2.4).

St.17. *Refuge* rhymes with *suis-je*. Here the problem is more complex. Although Chatelain[20] attests the use of the rhyme *i / ui*, he does not consider *u / ui*. The rhyme is evidently on *u* and we may consider this example as a weakness on the author's part or it may indeed have been a possible pronunciation of the 1st person singular of the present tense of *être*.

St. 21. *Ensemble* rhymes with *Anne*. The pronounciation of *a* and *e* is studied by Chatelain[21] in the context of the *ame / eme* group. The assimilation of this group is, according to Chatelain, attested in XIVth and XVth century authors. Although the problem is somewhat different here, I feel that the rule most probably applies and, in fact, reinforces the contention that this text bears the influence of the Picard dialect.

St. 23. *Annas, bras, Judas,* and *Cayphas* rhyme together, a perfectly normal occurrence in the XVth century when the last consonant was usually sounded, but one which might appear unusual to a XXth century reader.

St. 31. *Seuls* rhymes with *leups*. Here we have either an assimilation of *l* and *p* for the purpose of pronunciation, or a rhyme on the diphthong *eu*. In view of Chatelain's repeated remarks regarding the pronunciation of consonants at the end of lines, it would seem that the *s* at least was pronounced, whereas *p* was silent, and, indeed, we find in the *livre des trois eages*,[22] *temps* rhyming with *gens*. The *e* may have also been silent. (see st. 35).

St. 34. Herode rhymes with *s'aborde*. This is simply a case of metathesis *or/ro*, a not uncommon occurrence in Picardy (*Buvrage / bruvage* etc.).

St. 35. Volt rhymes with *mot*. Here undoubtedly the *l* is silent; a fact which reinforces the suggestion made for the rhyming of *seuls* and *leups* (st. 31).

St. 44. Veoir rhymes with *flechir, ferir, issir*. The rhyme is obviously on *ir*. As *veoir* cannot be counted as 3 syllables, since *eo* cannot diphthongize, we have obviously here a "rime pour l'oeil".

St. 45. Suffice rhymes with *crucifie*. I cannot find any example of a silent *c* in this position. The rhyme is, I believe, simply faulty.

St. 56. Here *scitifs* rhymes with *proffis, Juys* and *mis*. The rhyme is obviously intended to be on *is* and *f* is treated as silent.

St. 71. Here we are faced with a double problem; the following words are meant to rhyme: *douce / angoisse / couche / bouche*. Chatelain[23] notes"...les deux articulations *s* et *ch* étaient alors moins eloignées l'une de l'autre qu'elles ne le sont aujourd'hui". This applies particularly to Picard texts. Thus it is not unusual for *ce, sse,* and *che* to rhyme. What is less defensible is to make *ou* and *oi* rhyme together and in the absence of further justification this must be construed as a weakness. It should none the less be noted that in Charleroi, to-day, the pronunciation of *angoisse* is *angouche*. Von Wartburg's FEW signals *angouche* in Boulonnais, at Créquy (district of Montdidier, Somme). At Saint - Pol - sur - Ternoise; it means: sharp and short pain.

D. Philological survey [24]

1. Morphology

No sauvement (5.5): The possessive form *no* for *nostre* is listed by Pope as one characteristic of the northern region.[25] Gossen also states[26] that while Francien had *nostre, vostre,* for the masc. sing., accusative, the Picard dialect used the weakened forms *no* and *vo*. This is therefore another example of the Picard features of the text.

Eut (16.2 and 23.4 and 6): Burguy lists *eut* as a Picard form of the preterite [27] while Gossen says *ot* and *eut* coexist among Picard authors.[28]

Such is the case, interestingly, in stanza 23 of our poem. In *ot livré*, however, *ot* is used as an auxiliary It may be significant that in *ot sué* (st. 13) and *n'y eut* (st. 16), the other two cases of the preterite of *avoir* occurring in this poem, *ot* is again an auxiliary, while *eut* is not. The small number of examples does not allow us to draw any definite conclusion as to the reasons for the poet's choices.

Sur lui imposon (29.6): This is obviously a third person plural; it is attested by Fouché, accented forms [ô] having been found in several areas of northern France for the third person plural, both in the present indicative and in the present subjunctive. Again, it should be noted that this form is still used to-day in Nivelles, Waimes and Faymonville. This form is found in the Liège writer, Jehan d'Outremeuse.[29]

Celle Vierge (71.1): The use of an apparent demonstrative, such as *celle* instead of an article, is a feature of "Moyen Picard", as attested by both Flutre and Gossen. "A côté de l'article *le*, le Moyen Picard possède un autre article, *che, chel, chez* derivé de l'adjectif démonstratif."[30] Gossen notes those forms in modern Picard, but only cites one in Old Picard.[31]

2. *Syntax*

Sané (20.3): One would expect a feminine ending. As Foulet notes, regarding the agreement of a past participle preceded by a direct object, "les règles d'accord du participe annoncent déjà l'usage moderne,"[32] but he hastens to add that the rules are not strictly adhered to. In this particular context, the apparent lack of consistency is explained by the requirements of the rhyme; the agreement rule is observed in *reprise* and *remise* (same stanza), which rhyme with each other, whereas *sané* rhymes with the masculine form *dampné*.

Vist, assist, interrogue, oyt, a dit (st. 24, whole): "passé simple", preterite and "présent historique" coexist within the same narration. This is not uncharacteristic of Middle French. Wilmet devotes an exhaustive study to this phenomenon,[33] concluding:

> "Engagée en Moyen Français, la dégradation du couple oppositionnel d'aspect formé par le passé simple et le passé composé s'est donc poursuivie jusqu'en français moderne. Le

libre choix d'un tiroir passé n'est toutefois pas total aujourd'hui encore".[34]

Adonc veissiez (25.1): I interpret this form as an imperfect subjunctive used in a conditional meaning. This use of the subjunctive was often preferred in Old French to the conditional.[35] It may be asked why *vissiez* is not used, since, as Fouché [36] points out, *veisse* had become *visse* during the early XIVth century: "...au XVè siècle, la réduction est un fait accompli, dans les dialectes autres que ceux du Nord et du Nord-Est." Thus the geographic location may have been a factor. Also Fouché adds: "Cependant l'*e* peut avoir été conservé dans la graphie", and gives several examples.[37]

3. *Lexicology*

This list includes words whose spelling, meaning or use is unusual either for the modern reader or in the context of common contemporary use. The words are given in the order in which they appear in the text.

Excerciter (1.2): This spelling is attested in the related noun *excercitement* found in Courci's *Histoire de la Grèce* (Ars 3689 f. 69, quoted by Godefroy).[38]

Pas (3.4): The place where one stands; an observation post; see Froissart *Chron.* V, 49, Kerv. "Les Engles restoient tout quoy sans yaus mouvoir de leur pas" (quoted by Godefroy).

Aprist (6.5): Godefroy indicates that *aprenement* can mean: teaching, although the word, in its verbal form, is not attested.

Office (6.5): Here, it certainly means Divine Office, Eucharist (cf. Med. Lat. *Officium*). This meaning is not attested by Godefroy but appears in Cotgrave[39] "also, Divine Service".

Enhorta (8.2): *Ennorter* or *enhorter*, defined as *conseiller* or *exhorter*, occurs in Froissart with the same spelling: "tant consilla et enhorta ..."(*Chron.*III, 351, Luce Ms. Amiens f.88); quoted by Godefroy who also lists *inhorter* and *enhorter* as Rouchi elements, thus confirming the geographical origin of the *Passion*.

S'eslonga (8.4): *S'eslonguer* is attested by Godefroy as signifying: to lie down; while *eslongner*, *esloignier*, and *eslongier* correspond to modern French *éloigner* or *s'éloigner*. *Eslongast* (without reflexive pronoun, but with to-day's reflexive meaning) is found in Froissart.

Lez (9.4): Side.

Transmis (10.1): is attested in Tobler-Lommatzsch[40] (sich verwandeln), but not in Godefroy who only gives *se transmettre*. However, he gives *transmuer* which, in the reflexive form, means: to go from one place to another. Cotgrave gives *transmettre*: to send from one place to another.

Incorpora (11.2): Penetrated himself with. In attestation of this meaning Godefroy cites Oliver de la Marche (*Mem.* I,4).

Angele (12.3): is attested by Huguet[41] and he quotes: "Ces mesmes poëtes...faisant de la nature angelique ainsi que de l'humaine, disent au feminin *Angele*". M. de la Perthe. *Epithètes*. 23 - 24.

Baisier (15.6): To kiss. Although *baisir* is more common at the time, and Gossen cites *basier* as the Rouchi form, he adds: "il faut croire que pour beaucoup de scribes picards les graphies *ai* et *a* étaient interchangeables".[42] It is also attested by Flutre.[43]

Osez (16.3): Godefroy gives *ose* only as a noun meaning: boldness. Cotgrave gives the verbal form: to be so bold as to do a thing.

Attrait (17.5): with the meaning of: having come nearer, is attested by Tobler-Lommatzsch: sich begeben; sich anschliessen.

Meleois (18.2): from the past participle of *maleïr* (to curse), i. e. the accursed.

Cremeur (19.4): Cotgrave gives this form as obsolete but Godefroy gives *cremor*, a form attested in the XIVth century and, in the XVth, in the introduction of La Marche's *Mémoires*. Dauzat[44] indicates that this form comes from popular Latin, the alteration being owed to Gaulish influence.

Sané (20.3): Healed (<*sanare*)

Entour lui font (21.2): They surround him. Godefroy gives *entourer*: to lock in a tower and *entour* (noun): circuit.

Buffiez (22.1): Slapped in the face. Derived from *bufar*: to buffet.

Ensement (23.1): Similarly.

Prologue (24.6): in the feminine is not attested.

Courchiez (25.2): angered. This is the equivalent of O. F. *Correcier*, lat. *corruptiare. In Liège one still hears to-day: *corcî*. *Perchier* (44.6) is also a Picard form. As regards *embracier* (15.3), both this form and *embrachier* are attested by Godefroy. In a text displaying marked Picard features, we might have expected the second form, but the rhyme with *baisier* was certainly a factor in the poet's choice.

Pulens (26.5): Dirty, foul.

Chetis (27.1): Slave, hence comtemptible.

Mainmise (28.4): Seizure, distraint (feudal law).

Averis (30.1): fulfilled.

Sacquant (34.2): (< *sakier): chasing, jostling. The etymology is variously given as: *Saccare from Lat. saccus: a sack, (FEW, Greimas, Grandsaignes d'Hauterive). For Delmotte, the Walloon form *Sakier* comes from Spanish *saccar*, but *sacquer* would come from Celtic *sacha* = pull.[44a]

Boutant (34.2): (< Frankish *botan*: to beat): pushing, jostling.

S'aborde (34.6): Accosts. Attested only as a noun by Godefroy. The verbal form *abordoier* is attested by Huguet: *s'aborder à quelqu'un*. (Lemaire des Belges, *Ill.* I.44; Fr. d'Amboise, *Dial.des Damoiselles*: I, 126.r.) Also attested as a verb in Tobler-Lommatzsch but not in the reflexive form.

L'enquesta (35.1); Godefroy attests the noun *enquestement* and the verb *enquerre*, whose past tense only is attested in *Perceval*. Huguet gives the meaning: to question (Des Periers *L'Andrie* I, l; and Beroalde de Verville, *Le Moyen de Parvenir* I, 260). Cotgrave gives the noun *enqueste*: an inquest, and [s'] *enquester*: to search, examine, question, inquire, ask. He also gives *enquesteur*: a searcher, an examiner, etc.... In our text, the meaning is: he questioned him.

Il rescout son sol (36.3): The usual sources are not helpful, except Cotgrave who has a verb *rescouer*: to shake often. The meaning is probably: he wagged his head. (It is interesting to note that Ms. N gives: *il tourna son col*.)

Reputoit (36.5): Considered him to be.

Navré (40.5): Wounded; according to Wartburg: <Old Norse *nafra*: to pierce through.

Attant (45.3): Adverbial locution meaning: at this point, thereupon (also spelt *a tant*).

Exemplaire (48.3): Attested by Godefroy: model.

Playez, chargiez, etc. (the whole of stanza 48): see also *humiliez* (4.3 etc.). This *z* does not indicate a plural, as the participles refer to *exemplaire*, and in the case of stanza 4, to *Seigneur*. This is a case where, according to Beaulieux,[45] *z* plays the part of a diacritical sign indicating *e* in a closed position.

Bouté (51.3): Pushed, jostled (<Frankish *botan*: to beat); see also (34.2).

Coeuvrechie (51.4): According to Godefroy (*Comp.* IX, 235c) this kerchief is "un voile de toile fine, de soie, de gaze".

Diffamer (53.1): To bring to shame.

Agrangoit (54.2): This form, given in all three manuscripts is not otherwise attested. Godefroy attests *agrandoier*.

Parceux (55.1): Past participle of *parcheoir*: to fall off;. here *fallen men*.

Se deffient (55.3): Disavow. This verb is recorded by Godefroy only in the active. The pronominal form is attested in the XVIth century only. (Melin de St. Gelais *Huitain*).

Scitifs (56.1): thirsty.

Avis (61.5): Here: reason, wisdom. Godefroy cites this meaning with J. de Condé *De l'amant trahi* 155 Scheler and *Un miracle de Notre Dame: Comment elle garda une femme d'estre arse* Théâtre Français au moyen âge, p. 345.

Gron (71.4): lap. This form is noted by Godefroy.

Labeurs (73.4): Godefroy notes that the word is used figuratively with the meaning of fatigue or suffering.

Forment (75.5): much, greatly (modern French: fortement).

4. *Dialect and Conclusions*.

It has been shown in this philological survey that, where a given form deviated from Middle French usage, a Picard, Walloon or Rouchi influence is usually evident. Because such deviations are relatively infrequent in this text, we would be inclined to describe the language of this poem as "picardisant" or Franco-Picard" as Elcock called it.[46]

If, however, the text originated in Bruges, long under Burgundian domination, but whose prevailing language was Flemish, how do we explain the use of a Franco-Picard dialect? Although during the XIVth and XVth centuries, French was used in Flanders for administrative purposes, no wholesale francization of the territory was attempted by its Burgundian rulers. On the contrary, Henri Pirenne notes that some of the dukes of Burgundy had Flemish tutors and that Charles the Bold spoke Flemish fluently.[47] In this connexion, Pirenne states that:

> "Le reproche adressé si souvent à la maison de Bourgogne d'avoir voulu systématiquement franciser les Pays-Bas, reçoit des faits un éclatant démenti. Si le français, déjà fort répandu dans les classes supérieures de la société depuis le XIIè siècle, devint nécessairement sous la nouvelle dynastie la langue du gouvernement central, il subit au contraire un recul dans l'administration interne des provinces flamandes".[48]

From the XIVth century onwards, French cultural influence began to wane in the Flemish provinces. But the use of French persisted, not only at court but also among the nobility and the richer families of the bourgeoisie "qui continuent d'envoyer leurs enfants l'apprendre dans les villes wallonnes."[49] Thus the Walloon influence on the French language spoken in Flanders is evident. Pirenne also cites a Jean de Dadizeele who, at the age of twelve, went to live in Lille then to Arras in order to learn French.[50]

The same author gives several examples of the reciprocal influence of Flemish and northern French dialects, through travel across the linguistic border for such occasions as archery competitions and the performance of plays: "de même qu'on entendait jouer des pièces en langue française dans les communes flamandes, des acteurs thiois exécutaient de leur côté des *Abelespeelen* dans les villes romanes du sud..."[51]

Yet in the next statement, the historian Pirenne seems to discount Picard influences:

> "Jusqu'au milieu du XIIIè siècle, la littérature d'expression française dans les Pays-Bas a été une littérature provinciale. Les dialectes employés par elle étaient le picard dans l'Ouest, le wallon proprement dit dans l'Est. Mais, à partir de cette date, c'est au français de France que recourent tous ceux qui

ambitionnent de bien écrire et de mériter les éloges des gens de goût."[52]

The key word is "ambitionnent." As Pirenne had pointed out earlier, young Flemings learned their French in neighbouring towns, where northern dialects were spoken, and thus their "ambition" may not have been fully realized; their French more than likely exhibited dialectal features.

The similarity of language used by the author of the *Passion* and by Froissart has been indicated repeatedly in our philological survey, since many language features of the *Passion* were attested by excerpts from Froissart's texts. It is interesting to note that, according to Elcock, Froissart was very much aware of his "Picardism" and that, when he transferred his allegiance from the Flemings to the French, he also took pains to express himself in elegant French.[53]

To sum up, there is no conflict between the Franco-Picard language of the present poem and its origin on Flemish soil. In the cosmopolitan cities of Flanders under the Dukes of Burgundy, with the rich cross-currents of literary and artistic talents which their courts attracted, the occurrence of linguistic exchanges and diversity should be accepted as part of the historical scene.

NOTES

1. Henri Chatelain, *Recherches sur le vers français au XVe siècle: rimes, mètres et strophes.* Paris (Champion), 1908, p. 235.

2. *Op. cit.*, p. 111.

3. A short examination of this poetic pattern based on the above-mentioned texts will be found in Appendix B.

4. Cp. Alfred Jeanroy, *Les origines de la poésie lyrique en France au moyen âge.* Paris (Champion), 1904, p. 364 ff.

5. Ernest Langlois, *Recueil d'arts de seconde rhétorique.* Paris (Imprimerie Nationale), 1902. Documents inédits sur l'histoire de France, série 5, vol. 8.

6. Molinet, *Arts de rhétorique*, p. 218.

7. Langlois, op. cit., p. LXXI.

8. *Ibid.*, p. 256.

9. *Ibid.*, p. LXXIV.

10. *Ibid.*, p.272.

11. H. Chatelain, *op. cit.* p. 252.

12. George Lote, *Histoire du vers français.* Paris (Hatier), 1955, livre VI, 2e section, ch. 2. p. 321.

13. *Cheus*: The even metre requires a disyllabic pronunciation of the *eu* although at that time the participle ending was in the process of changing to *u*. Fouché notes, however, that the spelling *eu* persisted even though the sound was changing and, furthermore, that in certain provinces and even among certain Parisians the disyllabic pronunciation persisted into the XVIIth century. See P. Fouché, *Morphologie historique du français. Le Verbe.* Paris (Klincksieck), 1967, p. 362.

14. E. Langlois, *op. cit.*, p. 201.

15. G. Lote, *op. cit.*, p. 323.

16. E. Langlois, *op. cit.*, p. 252.

17. *Ibid.*, p. 200.

18. See H. Chatelain, *op. cit.*, p. 33 ff.

19. See M. F. Anderson Jr., *Pierre Choinet, Le livre des trois eages, édition critique et commentée*. Doctoral Dissertation: University of California, Davis, 1975. vol. 1 p. 123.

20. See H. Chatelain, *op. cit.*, p. 14.

21. *Ibid.*, p. 26.

22. See F. M. Anderson, *op. cit.*, p. 124.

23. H. Chatelain, *op. cit.*, p. 68.

24. I am indebted to Prof. L. Tyler and Dr. R. Pinon for their helpful suggestions regarding this section of the chapter.

25. M. K. Pope, *From Latin to Modern French*. Manchester (U. P. Manchester), 1934, p. 238.

26. See C. T. Gossen, *Grammaire de l'Ancien Picard*. Paris (Klincksieck), 1970, p. 127.

27. G. F. Burguy, *Grammaire de la langue d'oil* Tomes I - III). Berlin, (F. Schneider et cie), 1853-6. see I, p. 246.

28. See C. T. Gossen, *op. cit.*, p. 130.

29. See P. Fouché, *op. cit.* pp. 8-11. See also J. Coppens, *Grammaire Aclote* [...] pp. 88-123; L. Remacle, *Le problème de l'ancien wallon*, p. 83 and, same author: *Syntaxe du parler wallon de la Gleize*, p. 36, n.1.

30. L. F. Flutre, *Le Moyen Picard d'après les textes littéraires du temps (1560-1660)*. Amiens (Société de linguistique picarde), 1960. P. 502. See also R. Debrie, "Nouvelles recherches concernant *chu* considéré comme article démonstratif en picard" in Revue de Linguistique romane", 43, 1979 pp. 63-78.

31. See C. T. Gossen, *op. cit.*, p. 122.

32. L. Foulet, *Petite syntaxe de l'ancien français*. Paris (Champion), 1967, p. 105.

33. M. Wilmet, *Le système de l'indicatif en moyen français*. Genève (Droz), 1970 p. 275 - 324.

34. *Ibid.*, p. 324.

35. See, for instance, *la Chanson de Roland*, line 3388: "La veissiez la terre si jonchiee" quoted by J. Anglade, *Grammaire élémentaire de l'ancien français*. Paris (A. Colin), 1965, p. 210.

36. P. Fouché, *op. cit.*, p. 348.

37. *Loc. cit.*

38. All references to Godefroy come from his *Dictionnaire de l'ancienne langue française* Paris (Vieweg). 1881 - 1902; New York (Kraus Reprint), 1961 under the word discussed.

39. R. Cotgrave; *A Dictionnarie of the French and English Tongues* [...] London, 1611.

40. A. Tobler, *Altfranzösisches Wörterbuch.* Ed. E. Lommatzsch. Berlin, (Weidmannsche Buchhlandlung), 1925 - 1960.

41. E. Huguet, *Dictionnaire de la langue française du seizième siècle.* Paris, (Champion-Didier), 1925 - 1967.

42. C. T. Gossen, *op. cit.*, p. 53.

43. See L. F. Flutre, *op. cit.*, p. 205

44. See A. Dauzat, *Nouveau dictionnaire étymologique.* Paris (Larousse), 1964.

44a. See A. J. Greimas, *Dictionnaire de l'ancien français* p. 576b; see also R. Grandsaignes d'Hauterive, *Dictionnaire de l'ancien français* [...] p. 525a, also, P. Delmotte, *Essai d'un glossaire* [...] pp. 614-618.

45. See C. Beaulieux, *Histoire de l'orthographe française.* Paris (Honoré Champion), 1967, vol. I, p. 162.

46. W. D. Elcock, *The Romance Languages.* London (Faber and Faber), 1960, p. 365.

47. See H. Pirenne, *Histoire de Belgique.* Bruxelles (Henri Lamertin), vol. II, 1908, p. 310.

48. *Ibid.*, p. 384.

49. *Ibid.*, p. 445.

50. *See loc. cit.*

51. *Ibid.*, p. 450. See also Albert Henry, *Wallon et Wallonie.* Bruxelles (La Renaissance du Livre) 1974.

52. *Ibid.*, p. 455.

53. See W. D. Elcock, *op. cit.*, p. 365.

SOURCES AND COMMENTARIES

The author of the present *Passion* has remained anonymous, at least in the extant manuscripts. Yet, as was so often the case in the XIVth and XVth centuries, he, or at any rate one of the scribes, has claimed to be indebted to St. Bonaventure.

Folios 103 - 182 of the Bibiothèque nationale manuscript Fonds Français 190 contains 38 devotional pieces introduced as: "Devotions ordonnez par Frere Bonaventure. Recueil de trente huit pieces devotes traduites ou imitees de St Bonaventure" and, on fol. 182, the *explicit* reads: "Ci finent les meditations de frere bonne aventure de l'observance sur les misteres de la passion Jhesu Crist notre seigneur et autrement".

This proemial indication of source is more misleading than helpful. All mediaeval commentators are largely indebted to their predecessors and their work is more often than not an anthology rather than an original contribution.[1] In the case of the life and Passion of Christ, most late mediaeval authors borrowed from St. Bonaventure's *Vita Christi*[2] and the pilfering took place, of course, without any acknowledgement.

It is therefore no wonder that the author of the *Heures de la Passion* studied here took inspiration from St. Bonaventure's *Vita Christi* but, in fact, being among good and crowded company, it proves nothing. Even Jean Sonet in his *Répertoire*[3] makes the same remark, going as far as calling the Heures de la Passion a "Paraphrase des Méditations de St. Bonaventure". He certainly went too far.[4]

Apart from biblical and patristic sources, the authors made use of traditional and popular beliefs and anecdotes which had accumulated through the ages around the Passion story. What, indeed, makes each text worthwhile and so moving, is the attitude that each author adopts towards the facts, the angle from which he sees them and the responses he hopes to arouse in his readers.

With such a relatively short text, it would seem that little would be left to its author if he were indeed beholden to so many sources. And yet, reading the text through, although the reader is immediately aware of certain borrowings, he is left with a strange sense of originality; of passionate concentration, and dedication to the suffering of Christ, quite unlike the numerous contemporary texts on the same subject. What gives it its poignancy? I found the answer in reading the text in the actual Boston manuscript. Here each Canonical Hour is preceded with a miniature in *grisaille* and the actual centre of each miniature is Jesus himself, in the various episodes of his Passion, until, prepared for burial upon the unction stone (his soul having already descended into hell), Mary, at the very end, becomes the focal point of the iconography (and of the story itself). There is indeed a very wonderful correspondence between text and illustration in the Boston manuscript, and I have never found this elsewhere to such an extent before.

Adopting the dictum of Protagoras, the Renaissance will say: "Man is the measure of all things" but here, at the very end of the Middle Ages, God is indeed the measure of all things. And God, made man, is not the triumphant Christ of the early Middle Ages, whose crown of thorns is a glorious diadem studded with gems; he is the suffering human being reminiscent of the poor footsoldier of the Burgundian wars, buffeted, sent from pillar to post, and beaten in the end - yes, such is the Christ of the *Passion*, who dies at the very end without our even getting a glimpse of the Resurrection - a "pauvre hère" of a God whose only triumph is his human dignity, so reminiscent of Villon's attitude in *La Ballade des Pendus*. And the author saw no one else but Jesus: all other persons appearing in the narrative are incidental, blurred, never really in focus. The text, interspersed with meditations, reminds the reader constantly of the sweet and heartbreaking humanity of Christ and at the same time, of the universal meaning of each episode of his Passion.

The most striking difference between this text and other XIVth or XVth century Passion texts is the complete disregard here for any episode not directly centered on Jesus. To give a few examples only (the text will be studied in detail below): the author has omitted Peter's denial, Judas' suicide, and the release of Barabbas.

In fact, the two stanzas of introduction set the tone - and the theme - of the whole piece: it is a call to be united to, and to meditate upon, the Passion. Of the scene in the guest-chamber we are given two very brief glimpses only: the washing of the feet and the institution of the Eucharist. In the former, the author retains the humility of Christ:

> Regarde pecheur / Comment ton Seigneur / S'est humiliez /...Il lave les piez. (st. 4)

This is also the aspect retained by Pseudo-Bonaventure:[5]

> inclinavit se summa maiestas et humiliavit se usque ad piscatorum pedes. (fol. 36 r.2)

What inclines me to believe that this idea of humility is not fortuitous but indeed borrowed from Pseudo-Bonaventure is the pun - whether it be intended or not - on the word *piscatorum* which in this text is rendered by *pecheur*: the word for fisherman (*piscator*) and sinner (*peccator*) being the same in French.

The author leaves aside all of Christ's teaching (he only says: 'il les enseigna'): the long Eucharistic prayer as reported by St. John (ch. 14) and the last teaching in the Garden of Olives (John chs. 15, 16 and 17). For him the time for Christ's teaching is no more; it is now the time for suffering and death.

The agony in the Garden of the Mount of Olives occupies three stanzas (11 to 13) and includes, of course, the sweat of blood, and the help of the angel. The episode of the sweat of blood remains close to the evangelical text (Luke 22, v. 44). The image of blood covering the ground is taken up in this text and, indeed by most commentators. It recurs no less than three times in this text: an understandable attitude in a century so used to bloodshed.

The appearance of an angel at Christ's side to comfort him is treated in a very interesting manner. The angel is named by certain commentators: Princeps Michael,[6] his help is very summarily indicated: *astitit confortans eum* (Ps. Bonaventure) or *astitit confortans in eo motu sensualitatis* (Ludolf of Saxony, who never misses a chance to add a gloss, spiritual, moral or doctrinal[7]). And in another version of the Pseudo Bonaventurine text[8] we read (fol. 31v.):

> Tunc angelus de celo apparuit et in uisione corporali assumpto humano corpore per modum servientis consolans eum.

and further on (fol. 33 v.):

> ...ab angelo confortatur in hoc paulominus minoratus ab eo: et reverenter ab eo consolationem suscepit.

If our text does not name the angel, it indicates his attitude:

> Tres reveramment / L'angele conforte / Jhesus humblement / Et benignement / Le rechoit et porte (st. 12).

(three adverbs indicative of personal devotion).

It is interesting to compare the beginning of stanza 13:

> Or oste Jhesus / De sa face jus / Le sang qu'ot sué

with Ps. Bonaventure's interpretation (fol. 34r.):

> uultum illum angelicum sibi lauat in torrente uel uestibus suis tergit.

In the first instance, Jesus wipes his face; in the second this is done by the angel. Grammatically our text is correct. The personal pronoun 3rd person singular (il: line 4) is understood and therefore must refer to Jhesus in line l. It is this very reason which made me decide in the *apparatus criticus* in favour of the BC reading *Jhesus*; against the N reading: *a Jhesus*; a reading which, as it happens, also agrees with the stemma. Did the scribe of Ms. N add *a*, unconsciously influenced by the reading from Ps. Bonaventure, which he very likely knew? We cannot rule out the possibility.

The waking up of his disciples; the kiss of Judas; the soldiers falling to the ground; the act of Peter and healing of Malchus: all these follow the gospels closely (stanzas 14 to 20). Yet a few incidents are worthy of notice.

First of all, in st. 14, Ms. B gives *vint*; Mss C and N, *vient*. Both are equally acceptable. But it would seem that B follows the evangelical text of St. Matthew (26, 46): *appropinquavit*, whereas the other two Mss follow the text of the second response for Maundy Thursday at Matins: *appropinquat*.[9]

If commentators of the Passion borrow from the liturgy - and ours does so more than once - they also borrow from the Old Testament; thus we read, st. 17:

Dittes lequel c'est / Que querrez de fait, /Dist nostre refuge.

Nowhere in the gospels is Jesus called *refuge*, but this appellation is commonly given to God, especially in the Psalms where, for instance, it occurs at least 14 times, and in several other places (Deuter.; 2 Sam.; Prov.; Jeremiah; etc.).

Stanza 18 presents an interesting problem: Jesus, according to St. John's Gospel (18, 4-8), twice asks of the soldiers coming to arrest him whom they seek. And they answer: 'Jesus of Nazareth'. Now, whereas in St. John the soldiers fall once and no mention is made of Jesus intervening in any way, in our text the soldiers fall twice and each time Jesus helps them to their feet. This double fall is not unknown in comparable mediaeval literature and Duriez mentions a double fall in seven German Passion plays and even a triple fall in five others.[10] But whereas in these plays the interpretation given is rather in the line of a triumph for Jesus (his powers are still intact, in a way), in our text the intention is quite different and makes us aware, once again, of the author's attitude: Jesus shows compassion to the fallen soldiers:

Ainsi par deux fois / Le doulz roy des roys / Les a relevéz (st. 18).

Throughout the text, the apparent helplessness of Jesus is counterbalanced by his obvious inward strength and majesty. Witness again this slightly tongue-in-cheek but very moving remark found in st. 16: as no one dares put a hand on Jesus,

> Tous ont cuer failly / N'y eut si hardy / Qui fust sy osez / De toucher a lui.

Judas who seemed to have judged his master according to his own criterion, looks on:

> Dont fut esbahy / Judas n'en doubtez.

The episodes of Peter cutting the servant's ear and his healing by Jesus follows, here again, the trend set by the author: utter concentration on the Saviour's power and kindness with equal disregard for attending circumstances. Yet the legend of a barbaric and ungrateful Malchus was well-established in the Middle Ages: Duriez has studied how Malchus in numerous Passion plays, insults Jesus and calls him a sorcerer for having healed him. He it is who slaps him in the face in Annas' house; he who pulls his hair and beard; he who prepared the holes in the cross and gives Jesus gall and vinegar to drink. Already in the XIIth century Pierre de Blois (+1208) had written in a *cantilena*:

> Nec habet arcam requiem / Malchus in Christi faciem /Jason in vasa Domini / Manus extendit impias.[11]

Then begins the dreary sequence of journeys and visits which will last through the night and the early morning. Jesus is sent from pillar to post, interrogated, beaten, derided. This covers a long portion of our text: stanzas 21 to 45, and extends from the end of Matins, through Lauds, Prime and Terce.

This long night of interrogations, suffering, insults, derision, is usually found in mediaeval dramas and - often enough - in devotional treatises, commentaries and "visions", to be an excuse to revel in the brutality and gross humour of which popular taste was fond: nothing was too gruesome, too explicitly revolting then. By contrast a sense of restraint prevails in our text.

St. 21 follows closely the johannic gospel 18, v.12: they "seized Jesus and bound him and led him to Annas...."

> Prins et lye l'ont / ....Et ainsi s'en vont / A la maison Anne.

To this statement the author adds only two discreet points, leaving it to us to imagine the anguish of the prisoner, as no detail is given: "puis entour lui font / Huans tous ensemble" and "Grief tourment lui font".

Avoiding the usual mediaeval controversies as to whether Jesus was interrogated by Annas, our author, with simple common sense, feels rightly that this episode was only an excuse to insult Jesus and make fun of him. There are four verbs in six short lines: *buffiez, laidengiez, batus, chassiez*: a lot to happen when one knows that Annas' and Caiaphas' houses were separated only by a courtyard.

John 18, v.24) says that Jesus was sent "bound unto Caiaphas". Again our author keeps closely to the gospel "lyé col et bras", a detail which occurs here and there in the Acts of Pilate (2nd Greek form) and probably indicates the wish of Annas to make the prisoner look like a beast. And with great commonsense, again, the author understands Caiaphas's mood: the seditious problem arising before the Passover is more likely to cause him worries than to bring him recognition. He writes.

Annas....Son Seigneur envoye / Au grant Cayphas / Qui n'en eut grant joye.(st. 23)

At this point we expect three accounts: that of the interrogation, complete with false witnesses and a number of heads of accusation; Peter's denial, and Judas' suicide. But our author is obviously not interested in the quibblings of lawyers and, anyway, Jesus is innocent. And again - the word recurs inevitably - with strong commonsense, the author dismisses the whole kangaroo court and their findings in 3 terse lines:

Quant Jhesus l'oyt / Le vray lui a dit / Sans longue prologue. (st. 24)

Then the subject is dismissed. How different from the general run of mediaeval commentators!

The second and third accounts are just completely ignored. The author looks at Jesus and at him alone. He is not interested in Caiaphas [12] rending his garments (Matt. 26, v.65 and Mark 14, v.63), only in the issue concerning Jesus: "Dignes est de mort" (st. 25). On one side the silent accused, on the other the mad crowd, thirsty for blood: *courchiez, demener fort, enragiez* etc. (st. 25).

The end of Matins and the whole of Lauds (6 stanzas: 26 - 31) are perhaps the most heartbreaking. If, as I intend to show further on, the text was to be used at the appropriate time, that is, as far as Lauds is concerned, at dawn, then the contrast between the promise of a spring morning and the lonely suffering of the prisoner is unbearable. Stanzas 26 to 29 in fact, closely follow the gospel narrative. The same elements are there: the spitting, buffeting, blindfolding, smiting, insults, revilings. The only element culled from popular tradition and used by most commentators which he also adopts, is that the soldiers pull Jesus' beard. In this instance, he calls him the "tres amoureux": the all-loving, thus following his practice of contrasting Christ's gentleness with his torturers' callousness. But the focal point of that night of suffering is, in fact, the loneliness of Jesus. The stanza is placed, strategically, at the end of Lauds and just before Prime: thus, any of the contemporary perusers of the text who might have been tempted to get excited with the reading of four stanzas of tortures - and this was the common reaction in the XVth century: witness the numerous accounts of Passion play audiences - are suddenly faced with the following words:

> Ilz s'en sont fuiz / Com tous esbahis / Et tu ez tout seuls/Entre ces rabis / Comme les brebis / Sont entre les leups. (st. 31)

Such a reader would automatically have to identify himself with those who fled, the so-called friends of Jesus, whom he had predicted would be "scandalized":

> ....Scandelis / Seront tes amis / En la nuit prochaine. (st. 30)

(this being an adaptation of Matthew 26. v.31 and Mark 14, v.27). About this dereliction, Pseudo-Bede[13] writes: "Dominus...sederit inter inimicos quia derelictus a suis discipulis et amicis".

This stanza 31 is interesting on another count. Nowhere in the Passion narrative of the evangelists is the metaphor of the lamb and the wolf used. The only biblical reference likely to have influenced our author is found in Matt. 10, v. 16: "I send you as sheep in the midst of wolves". Yet it is to be found in almost every mediaeval commentator:

> ....o magister bone, agnus innocens, quomodo ibas inter lupos.[14]

and again:

> *Et ministri Iudeorum accesserunt* sicut lupi ad agnum.[15]

also:

> Jhesus estoit devant Pilate comme un aignel devant le leup.[16]

The seven stanzas of Prime describe Christ's first appearance before Pilate (2 st.) and the appearance before Herod (5 st.). Although our text follows the gospels closely, it is very selective. By comparison, our text develops the episode at Herod's palace much more than the gospels do. Of the three heads of accusation mentioned in the gospels, namely that Jesus perverted the nations, that he forbade giving tribute to Caesar, and that he was Christ, a King,[17] we learn nothing; the author mentions only that ils "l'ont accusé" (st.32) and: "Jhesus faussement / Cy accusé ont" (st. 33). We have noticed that tendency in our author before: this is no longer the time for quibblings or even for Jesus' teachings. Jesus' remarkable answer to Pilate[18] is dismissed in three lines.

> A l'accusement / Le vray Innocent / Bien pou y respont (st. 33)

The interview with Herod is, of course, of a very different nature: it is no longer a battle of wits, intellectual sparrings: we are back to plain suffering, and this is what the author wants us to be inescapably aware of. Once again, what the gospel describes as lengthy questioning is rendered in our text by: "Moult fort l'enquesta". Stanza 37 takes up the episode of the white robe. The controversy arose around the translation of ἐσθῆτα λαμπρὰν (Luke XXIII, 11) which can mean either white or sumptuous, gorgeous. That mad people wore a white vestment was a custom regularly endorsed by the commentators:

> "Alba ergo veste Herodes induit Christum quia haec vestis [....] erat morionum et stultorum. Suggillavit ergo hac veste Herodes Christi stultam ambitionem, quod scilicet stolide ex fatuitate Judeae regnum affectasset, et ambivisset".[19]

In his commentaries on the Passion, Ludolf of Saxony [20] discourses at length on the meaning of the white vestment:

> (de prima in Passione Domini): Herodes eum [....] illusit, induendo veste alba: et hoc in derisionem et signum illusionis, sicut fatui solent aliqua veste ludicra indui, qua cognoscantur ab aliis".

He recalls - "ut dicitur" - that this vestment resembled the scapular of a religious habit, but without the hood.

> Unde Ambrosius [in cap. 23 Lucae]: Non ociosum quod veste alba induitur ab Herode immaculatae tribuens indicia passionis quod agnus Dei sine macula peccata mundi susciperet.

In the mind of the author of the present *Passion*, this episode, succintly retold, is designed to arouse in us a sense of gratitude for the price paid by Christ for our redemption. To the derisory: *De lui se gabboit*; *desguisement, par derision* ...the author opposes:

> Regarde [....] comment le tout bon / Nostre amour achate.

The important word here is, of course, *achate*. Jesus buys us back not only through his physical, but also through his mental suffering. The other reading for this word is *embrace* which singularly weakens the theme, since, in this case, it does not involve the reader in Christ's suffering.

The Hour of Terce is concerned with the flagellation, the purple garment, the reed and crown of thorns, the *ecce homo* and the condemnation. In this, the author follows Matthew closely (27, v.26-30) as far as the crowning of thorns and mocking by the soldiers, then he picks up the narrative from John (19, v. 5-6). All the same, two elements are derived from tradition and liturgy if not from the gospels. The first is the fact that, for the scourging, Jesus was attached to a pillar or column. This tradition is well-established and constantly referred to [21] and has a special place in the Lenten liturgy:[22]

> Salve columna nobilis / Christi dolorum conscia/ ...

The second element is the fact that Jesus was scourged naked, whereas the gospels are agreed that they stripped him after the flagellation and before arraying him in a scarlet robe. The scourging of Jesus naked is upheld by St. Birget in her *Revelations*.[23] That our author was strongly influenced by Birget's *Revelations* seems certain: he concludes (st. 41) the narrative of the scourging by a cosmic vision:

> .....regarde embas / De song sang verras / La terre couverte.

- an obvious reminiscence of:

ou il alloit, la terre paroissoit teinte de sang.[24]

The mock worshipping of the torturers follows the text by St. Matthew, as I said earlier, with the exception of the spitting which is not mentioned in this context.

When the author goes on to follow St. John's text, he again leaves out the last wranglings between Pilate and the crowd (John 19, v. 4 and first part of 5) in order to concentrate on the issue of all this suffering:

Mais la gent vilaine / Crie a voix hautaine:/ "On le crucifie".(st. 45)

In fact, the Hour of Sext opens with the harrowing injustice of the death-sentence: "La dure sentence, crueuse et injuste ....". Sext takes the narrative from the stripping of the purple until the nailing on the cross. Again all extraneous episodes are omitted: the author concentrates exclusively on Jesus.

The first episode, that of the stripping of the purple, is mentioned solely for the suffering that Jesus must endure through the reopening of his wounds:

Grant doleur lui firent / Mais pou en sentirent / Selon que je sens (st. 47).

Our text mentions the further insults that Jesus has to suffer while carrying the cross. This element is absent from the gospels, but quite common in Passion poems[25] and plays[26] and can also be found in St. Birget.[27]

Although our text explains that Jesus was too weak to carry his cross (st. 49), it does not refer to the help given by Simon of Cyrene, but rather this remark serves to introduce Christ's mother to the Passion narrative: Mary suffers to see her son struggle under the weight of the cross. Yet, there is no reference to a formal meeting between Jesus and his mother (an episode very commonly exploited by poets, commentators and mystics alike). In fact, it becomes clear here that the tone of the narrative is unusually restrained: the author lets the barest facts speak for themselves, with a minimum of pathos quite uncommon in the XVth century. Here, the falls of Jesus are not mentioned, and neither are the meeting with the daughters of Jerusalem, the encounter with Veronica, the *Improperia* as they appear so heart-rending in the Good Friday liturgy and, indeed, in most mediaeval texts.

We are now on Mount Calvary and, once again, Jesus is stripped of his clothes. (This, by the way, is the seventh time that Jesus is either stripped or re-clothed). As in the previous instance, the author describes how the Saviour's blood flows when the wounds are re-opened:

> Quant on devestoit / L'abit qui tenoit / A ses dignes plaies/
> Tout son corps saignoit /.....(st.50).

this expression is strangely akin to that found in the Brixen Passion Play (lines 2449 - 50):[28]

> Ich wil dier so grausam dein Rockh ab ziechen / Das sich das pluet aus den wunden mues schmiegen.

Stanza 51 must surely be the most moving of the whole text:

> Celle au cuer courchié / A tant tournoié / Sacquié et bouté /
> Qu'a d'un coeuvrechie / Couvert et muchié / Son humanite.

Needless to say, this episode is not to be found in the gospels, yet it is not uncommon in mediaeval texts. In some cases, this service is rendered to Jesus by someone who happens to be on the scene. Here is St. Birget's vision:

> Or mon fils estant là nud comme il estoit nay, lors un accourut luy apportant un voile, duquel se couvrit ses hontes, avec grande ioie interieure.[29]

- but it is commonly Mary who performs this act of mercy for her son.

Ps. Bonaventure reports the incident, differently expressed, in various versions. Here are two of them:

> Sed super omnia tristabatur mestissima mater: quia dilectum filium: sic ignominiose conspicit denudatum. Unde ut dicitur. Accessit pia mater et filio suo approximans uelo sui capitis eum cinxit: atque uelauit.[30]

and:

> Accelerat igitur mater, et approximat filio, amplexatur et texit eum velo capitis sui.[31]

This last text is reminiscent of Ludolf of Saxony's interpretation:

> Tristatur autem supra modum, quia eum videt sic nudatum.
> Accelerat igitur mater, et filio suo approximat, et uelo capitis sui eum cingit et uelat.[32]

The incident is also reported in Ps. Bede:

> Sed mater ejus amantissima velum suum, quod habebat in capite suo, posuit circa eum plena anxietate, et involvit locum verecundum.[33]

Ps. Anselm gives a very vivid account of the episode:

> Cum venissent ad locum Calvariae ignominiosissimum, ubi canes et alia morticina projiciebantur, nudaverunt Jesum unicum filium meum totaliter vestibus suis, et ego exanimis facta fui; tamen velamen capitis mei accipiens circumligavi lumbis suis.[34]

And finally, here is a poetic rendering of the episode taken from the *Livre de la Passion:*

> Sa glorieuse chere mere / Qui soufroit douleur si enmere/
> C'on ne le pourroit raconter / Un sien queuvrechef fist geter /
> Sus le devant de son dous fis.[35]

In this version Mary uses her veil but asks someone to cover her son with it.

The lengthy controversy as to whether Jesus was crucified *sublime* [36] or *humi* [37] is far from resolved in our text. The opinion of the Church Fathers and the mystics is highly divided and S. Birget, in her *Revelations* sees the first form in I, 10 and the second in VII, 15.

Our text is extremely baffling on this point. St. 52 (the last of Sext) describes him thus:

> Regarde Jhesus / Sur la croix pendus / Les membres tirer /
> Tant fort estendus / Et de cloux agus / Piez et mains cloer.

In this stanza, Jesus is in the process of being crucified and the verb *pendus* would seem to indicate that the extension of the arms and legs and their nailing took place as Jesus was in a vertical position.

Yet, stanza 53 (the first of None) runs:

> Pour plus diffamer / Le vont eslever / Entre deux larrons.

If we take the events in sequence, Jesus has been nailed to the cross in stanza 52. If then the soldiers "are about to raise him" in stanza 53, it follows that Jesus was nailed on the ground, which forms a contradiction with what has been discussed before.

I hope I am not distorting the text if I give the following explanation: Let us note again that the first interpretation comes at the end of a Canonical Hour, and the second at the beginning of the next Canonical Hour. If, as I demonstrate elsewhere,[38] the text was used liturgically, stanza 52 was followed by certain prayers (for the dead, etc.) and whoever was using the text in that manner reconvened some time later for the Hour of None. It seems reasonable to think that, the crucifixion being the high point of the Passion narrative, the author would want to start with a reminder of this episode. He therefore picks up the thread of the narrative at the previous stanza, but this time the object of the meditation is no longer the process of the crucifixion, but the shame brought to Jesus as he has to suffer between two thieves; indeed he ends the stanza with the following exhortation:

Ce fait mediter / Devons sans cesser / Si nous sommes bons (st. 53).

All in all, therefore, I incline towards a crucifixion *sublime* in our text.

Following his well-established custom of concentrating the narrative strictly on Jesus, the author mentions the two thieves but no more; their addresses to Jesus and his answer are not reported. As I said earlier, the only reason for mentioning the thieves is that it represents one more humiliation for Jesus.

According to the mediaeval tradition, and especially as found among the mystics, our author describes the nails. Was Jesus crucified with three or with four nails? Duriez[39] has established that those who favour a crucifixion *humi* opt for three nails and the others for four. It seems then that, according to this text, Jesus would have been crucified with four nails.[40] But whatever the number of nails may be, all authors insist on the gruesome horror of the nailing. A great number of mystery plays (where visual appeal was an important factor) show the nails being blunted (sometimes by Malchus!) as more likely to inflict greater suffering on the victim. Not so with mystical writers: Ps. Anselm, for instance[41] describes the nailing of the feet with a "clavum acutissimum", and in the present text the author mentions some "clous agus".

A great deal of the suffering would undoubtedly have been caused by the weight of the body dragging on the limbs, and the loss of blood. All mediaeval authors, dramatic and otherwise, describe that suffering. Stanza 54 describes both the suffering and the loss of blood:

> Son corps qui pesoit / Les treus agrangoit / De ses piez et mains / Du sang qu'en yssoit / Et aval couloit / Le mont en est tains.

This text is probably closest to that of Ps. Anselm:

> Et cum erectus fuisset, tunc propter ponderositatem corporis omnia vulnera lacerata sunt et aperta, et tunc primo sanguis de manibus et pedibus copiosius emanavit.[42]

The same idea is developed in both Ps. Bonaventure and Ludolf of Saxony in a very similar phraseology:

> ex magnis illis scissuris et fontibus saluatoris: copiosi undique riui sanguinis perfluxerunt.[43]

and:

> Ita autem levatio non dubium, quin maximi doloris fuerit, eo quod tunc lacerabantur uulnera manuum et pedum ex ponderositate corporis: profluxeruntque copiosi riui sanguinis undique ex illis magnis scissuris et fontibus saluatoris [....] et terra per sanguinem decurrentem similiter mundatur.[44]

The last three lines of stanza 54 represent the third mention of the Saviour's blood covering the earth (see st. 11 and 41). Here the text is closest to Ps. Bede:

> Et statim cum clavi grossissimi immittuntur, sanguis incipit manare, et per crucem fluere usque at terram.[45]

Following his usual policy for economy in the use of words, the author manages in st. 55 to combine an indirect reference to Jesus' first Words on the Cross: "Father, forgive them; for they know not what they do" (Luke 23 v.34) with a subject for meditation: let us put our trust in him who prays for his torturers.

He also uses the same technique in stanzas 56 and 57. First, (st.56) the fifth Word of Jesus: "I thirst" (John 19, v.28) giving a mystical meaning: Jesus thirsts to redeem us (an interpretation extremely common in the Middle Ages);[46] then (st. 57) combining the last Words of Jesus: "Father, into thy hands I commend my spirit" (Luke 23, v.46) with a meditation on the anguish of Jesus, as both God and man.

We see that our author cites only three of the seven Words of Jesus on the cross. He leaves out the message to the good thief (already discussed earlier); the message to his mother and St. John; the words "My God, my God, why hast thou forsaken me?" and "it is finished". It is curious that he omits the third and fourth Words, considering, in the first case, the obvious devotion of the author for Mary and his compassionate treatment of her part in the Passion, and also the obviously dramatic appeal of the fourth Word, so much in line with the author's attitude to the Passion narrative. To this puzzle, I can find only one answer: A great deal happens that has to be covered traditionally within the confines of None and, among other events, the Seven Words. Our author was restricted by the structure he had chosen[47] to devote only seven stanzas to None, a "Little Hour". We may think that it is regrettable he had to eliminate some important points of the Passion narrative, but we can only acknowledge that, within the strictures required, he made a wise choice. Stanza 58 starts with the adverb *angoisseusement*, probably indicating in the author's mind the mood of the actual Sixth Word. The same is probably true of two lines of st. 57 interpreting the fourth Word:

La paine et misere / Et l'angoisse grande

This leaves the third Word unaccounted for. Whatever his devotion to Mary, the episode is, after all, extraneous to the actual Passion and, in fact, an enclave of comfort and relative warmth in an otherwise bleak and harrowing narrative. And the author wants to keep it such.

The second part of st. 58, and st. 59, deal with the descent into Hell. This episode is not mentioned in any of the Gospels, but is alluded to in Ephes. 4, v.9 and in 1 Peter 3, v.19, and of course, appears in the Creed. But, his main source was, directly or indirectly, most probably the gospel of Nicodemus, a text well-known and widely used in the Middle Ages.

> Et ecce subito infernus contremuit, et portae mortis et serae comminutae et vectes ferrei confracti sunt.[48]

It should be noted that this episode is only found in the Latin form 2nd version, Part II. But whereas this text goes to great lengths to relate the intercourse of Jesus with the multitude of the inhabitants of Hell, starting with Adam, our text is far more reserved:

> En ce lieu trouva / Les sains qu'il ama / ..... Il les consola

The Gospel of Nicodemus speaks of the compassion of Jesus, of his affectionate greeting to Adam. Was this our author's only source? I have found only one other: in his Meditations for Holy Saturday, Ludolf of Saxony writes:

> Per seipsum ad inferna descendit, et non ut servos, sed ut amicos Dominus omnium eos uisitauit, et ibidem usque ad Diem Dominicum,(*sic*) prope auroram cum eis stetit.[49]

This corresponds almost word for word to Ps. Bonaventure's rendering in ch. 85. Both Ps. Chrysostom[50] and Ps. Anselm [51] relate the incident, but limit themselves to the breaking of the Gates of Hell. That our author was aware of Ps. Anselm's text seems likely since:

> [....] Son esperit rend [....] lequel [...] en enfer descend (st. 58)

corresponds to Ps. Anselm's: *Anima Christi descendit*. This incident ends the Hour of None.

Vespers embrace the trembling of the Earth; the Longinus episode and the descent from the Cross; but, underlying all this, it is really the Passion of Mary which we are given to meditate upon: the *Marien-klagen*. The Passion of Jesus is over but not that Our Lady. Out of 12 stanzas, five are exclusively devoted to Mary's suffering. The cult of The Virgin Mary had such a considerable importance in the Middle Ages that it outlived the courtly love sung by the *troubadours*, the *trouvères* and the *Minnesänger*. Indeed all devoted some of their most beautiful love poems to Our Lady and, in 1423, the Synod of Cologne instituted a new solemnity: The Office of the Compassion of Our Lady.[52]

I shall first take the stanzas relating to Mary's compassion, and deal afterwards with the three episodes mentioned above.

Stanzas 62, 63, 65, 70 and 71 are devoted to Our Lady. The first three depict Mary at the foot of the Cross. The other two concern the subject usually referred to as the *Pietà*.

Mary at the foot of the cross, swooning in the arms of St. John, is a subject often used by mediaeval painters. In the Boston Ms. both text and miniature agree in depicting Mary, not as fainting, but rather as burdened by sorrow, humped upon herself, swollen with grief:

> O Vierge Marie / Tu fus moult marrie / Au pied de la crois

and the author adds:

> Du sang ez mouillie / Du doulx fruit de vie / Qui est roy des roys. (st. 62)

This reference - once again to the Saviour's blood - finds an echo in Ps. Anselm:

> Ego autem induta fui quadam veste, qua mulieres regionis illius uti solent, qua tegitur caput et totum corpus, et est quasi linteum; et fuit ista vestis tota respersa sanguine.[53]

Mary is covered with the blood shed by the Son of Life, the King of Kings; but she weeps pitifully for her *child* hanged on a gibbet; she begs for him to be brought down and returned to her (st. 63). This is a true echo of the *Stabat Mater*, poignant and pitiful:

> Stabat Mater dolorosa / Juxta crucem lacrimosa / Dum pendebat filius.

But Mary's sufferings are not yet over: her son's side is gashed open by Longinus' spear. The episode occupies st. 64 to 68 but, apart from Longinus' miraculous cure (to which we shall return later) the author concentrates on Mary's suffering:

> Quant sa lance ostoit / Du coste yssoit / Sang en habondance / Marie le voit / Qui dueil en avoit / Creez sans doubtance. (st. 65)

Stanzas 70 and 71 end Vespers. Once again, they are devoted to Mary's Compassion: Joseph of Arimathaea and Nicodemus comfort the Virgin as they are about to free Jesus from the cross. And Mary in great torment receives her son in her lap and presses him to her, the *Pietà*:

> Celle Vierge douce / En moult grant angoisse / Son filz mort rechoit / En son gron le couche / Les yeux et la bouche / Souvent lui baisoit. (st. 71)

This most pitiful episode is echoed in the majority of mediaeval writers: it is indeed the epitome of Mary's Passion. Studying the *Pietà* in religious art, E. Mâle writes:

> Cette figure de la mère portant sur ses genoux le cadavre de son fils résumera chez nous, pendant le XVe et le XVIe siècle, toute la Passion de la Vierge".[54]

Our author was certainly aware, here again, of Ps. Anselm's dialogue with the Virgin:

> Exspectabam quando brachium solveretur, ut tangerem et deoscularer, sicut et feci; et cum depositus esset de cruce, posuerunt [...] Et ego caput ejus in sinum meum recipiens amarissime flere coepi [...][55]

The same descriptions are found in Ludolf of Saxony[56] but the nearest is, without doubt, in Ps. Bonaventure, this probably being the closest borrowing by our author from the *Meditationes*:

> Hii igitur nobiles viri ad virginem gloriosam accedentes et amicabilibus verbis salutantes et afflictam consolantes coram eidem eorum adventus exponunt flebili nihihominus compassione secum gementes.[57]

This is very closely rendered by our author as:

> Ilz vont saluer / Et reconforter / La tres glorieuse (st. 70)

and:

> Regarde comment / Joseph et sa gent / Et Nycodemus / Compassiblement / Et piteusement / Regardent Jhesus. (st. 69)

Further on, our author is obviously inspired again by the same commentator:

> [...] venerandam illam saepius deosculabat faciem. Tota quoque plena suspiriis et crebros edens singulariter hunc ulneribus pedum nunc manuum frigida oscula defrigebat.[58]

In our text, this passage is given in st. 71, quoted above.

As I said earlier, three episodes run parallel to Mary's Passion for Vespers: the trembling of the earth; the intervention of Longinus; and the descent from the cross.

The first one is not connected with the Passion in that, as shown earlier, the author had only chosen episodes directly related to the suffering of Jesus. It is, in fact, the only such episode in the whole text and it is almost vain to speculate on the author's reasons for such a choice. St. 60 reports the cosmic disturbances very much in the same terms as the gospels:

"A darkness came over the whole land ... the sun's light failing" (Luke 23, v.44-45)[59] is rendered by: "soleil eclipsa"; "and the earth did quake; and the rocks were rent" (Matt. 27, v.51) is rendered as: "Les pierres fendirent / La terre trembla"; "they feared exceedingly" (Matt. 27,v.54) is very faithfully rendered as: "Dont de ce fait la / Pluiseurs s'esbahirent".

Now, the following stanza (st. 61) brings in St. Denis, and a confusion arises - common enough in the Middle Ages - between Dionysius the Pseudo-Areopagite, a sixth century Syrian, and St. Denis who, with his companions Rusticus and Eleutherius, came down from Montmartre carrying his head in his arms. The former Dionysius in a letter supposedly written to Polycarp[60] tells how he witnessed from Heliopolis in Egypt, the solar eclipse that took place at the time of the death of Jesus. The confusion has, in fact, its origin in the Golden Legend:

> De Sanctis Dionysio, Rustico et Eleutherio: "In die igitur dominicae passionis, cum tenebrae factae fuissent super universam terram, philosophi, qui erant Athenis, non potuerunt hujus causam in causis naturalibus invenire. [...]. Statim Dionysius cum Damari uxore sua et tota familia baptizatus est ....".[61]

The second episode pertaining to Vespers is that of Longinus piercing Jesus' side with his spear, and the subsequent miracle. It occupies four stanzas (64 - 67). The first two stanzas are a faithful rendering of the johannic account:

One of the soldiers pierced his side and straightaway there came out blood and water (Jo. 19. v.34) but the name of the soldier, his blindness and cure, are not given in the Scriptures.

His name appears in the Acts of Pilate:

Et lancea latus ejus perforavit Longinus miles (XVI, 7).

Tradition has it that Jesus' blood ran along the haft of the spear and that, having accidentally rubbed his eyes with the Saviour's blood, Longinus recovered his sight.

The incident is not mentioned in Ps. Bonaventure, but recurs almost *verbatim* in many other authors;[62] I shall limit myself here to citing Ludolf of Saxony:

> Quid autem eum lanceavit, cum fere caligassent oculi eius prae senectute et casu, vel potius nutu diuino: sicut et lanceauit, licet nesciens, sanguine Christi, per lanceam defluente oculos tangeret: continuo clare uidit, et protinus illuminatus in Christum credidit;[63]

and the Golden Legend:

> De Sancto Longino: "Longinus fuit quidam centurio, qui cum aliis militibus cruci domini adstans jussu Pylati latus domini lancea perforavit et videns signa, quae fiebant, solem scilicet obscuratum et terrae motum, in Christum credidit. Maxime ex eo, ut quidam dicunt, quod cum ex infirmitate vel senectue oculi ejus calligassent, de sanguine Christi per lanceam decurrente fortuito oculos suos tetigit et protinus clare vidit."

This episode is separated from the arrival of Joseph of Arimathaea and Nicodemus - and the descent from the cross - by one stanza of meditation which is quoted here in full:

> Paine toy, labeure / Jour, nuit, a toute heure. / Entre en son coste / S'en luy fais demeure / Dy et si t'asseure / Qu'as repos trouvé (st. 68)

That the author remembered John's Gospel is almost certain:

> We will come unto him and make our abode with him (Jo. 14, v.23)

But Ludolf of Saxony's words are a much more direct source of inspiration: commenting on Augustine's *in manuali* cap. 23, the Carthusian writes:

> Longinus, inquit, aperuit mihi latus Christi lancea, et ego intraui: ibi requiesco securus.[64]

I have already commented on stanzas 69 and 70 as they pertain to Mary's Passion. This episode, which is almost always the subject of a miniature in Books of Hours, is here disposed of in three terse lines; it would seem that the important event to be retold is not the actual descent from the cross but, indeed, Mary's suffering, and this is sustained by the stanza which follows: the scene of the *Pietà*

The atmosphere which pervades Vespers, namely the Passion of Mary, is just as noticeable at Compline. The actual subjects are the embalming, shrouding and burial of Christ, but, in fact everything relates to Mary's Passion.

The Gospels' narrative regarding the entombment is extremely sparse. The synoptics[65] only relate that Joseph took the body away, wrapped it in a cloth, and laid it in a tomb. They do not even mention Nicodemus. John's narrative[66] is more elaborate and mentions that Nicodemus brought the spices. As to Mary, only Mark (15, v.47) clearly mentions her presence at the sepulchre, but without commentary. It is, therefore, easy to see the extent to which mediaeval devotion enlarged and dramatised the role of Our Lady in the last phase of her son's Passion. Commentators, mystics and dramatists give Mary a very active part in the Passion, particularly after Jesus' death when, as I have shown earlier, it really becomes her Passion or, as it has also been rightly called, her Compassion.

The preparation of the Body and the entombment which form the subject of Compline (and conclude this text) follow, yet with restraint, the usual mediaeval narratives: a development of John 19, v.40, where he writes that Jesus was buried according to Jewish custom. The body is washed and dried and surrounded by "espices et fleurs et bonnes odeurs" (st. 73) (St. John mentions myrrh and aloes); it is then wrapped in a shroud and taken to the tomb accompanied by keening:

"Et en grans labeurs / de plaintes et pleurs / L'ont ensevely" (st. 73).

"Par gemissement / au plourer forment / l'un l'autre provocquent" (st. 75).

But it is Mary's role which in our text, is so interesting, as it departs markedly from all other usual sources. Here Mary does not help in the burial of her son; she does not beg to be buried with him nor does she make a plea to other mothers. Three stanzas give us a picture of Mary, stunned with grief, but silent and immobile in her sorrow. Indeed, the poignancy is such as may have been born from experience of personal bereavement by the author.

St. 74 follows the shrouding of Jesus and Mary helplessly witnessing the scene which has inexorably unfolded before her:

[...] plouroit / Quant de lui avoit / La veue perdue.

The time for long discourses or exhortations is over. Her grief is restrained, discreet, humble; she wishes, *if it were possible*, to see him "en sa face nue".

For one last time (st. 76) her son is laid in her arms and the style used is inescapably reminiscent of a mother holding a baby (indeed, we are also reminded of old Simeon's prophecy).

Marie a receu / Son filiz en ses bras

but from her, no sighs escape, no outward signs of sorrow. We know of her grief through other persons present:

Ceulx qui l'ont veu / De pitie esmeu / Peuent dire: Hellas.

Now the "deux vrais amis" (Joseph and Nicodemus) have also departed. The stage is utterly silent. This is the uncanny silence which follows great catastrophes. Mary is alone with her "Dueil multipliant", nothing can be done as she leaves behind "her sweet beloved son". We are not given the slightest glimpse of the Resurrection. Hope is not visible. Death and misery prevail. Utter loneliness and great desolation. The stage is empty.

In conclusion, the study of this text has shown that the author's concern lay less in a theological or even mystical discourse on the meaning of the Passion, than on a practical and personal understanding of the sufferings of Jesus, our brother and friend and, whenever he relied on other writers, he invariably chose those who favoured this tendency.

The Franciscan spirituality is everywhere apparent in this *Passion*, as I have shown. Yet, I do not think this is the complete picture. The psychological realism which is ever present, the worship of a human Christ, as well as a repeated invitation to meditate on the Passion as a means of emulating piety and sanctity, all these are the hallmark of the "Devotio moderna"[67] whose ideals had been flourishing in the Netherlands and in Flanders since the end of the XIVth century. By the end of the following century the Brothers and Sisters of Common Life, under the spiritual guidance of men such as Gerard de Groote, Gerlac Peters and Thomas à Kempis, lived in well-nigh one hundred communities, devoting their lives to the spiritual aims mentioned above and earning a living by copying books. That the present text, whose Picard and Flemish origins have been abundantly proved, came within the sphere of their influence is therefore not surprising.

NOTES

1. See N. Marzac, *Richard Rolle* [...]Paris 1968, p. 91.

2. According to J.G. Bougerol, Jean "de Caulibus" may have been the author of the pseudo-Bonaventurine *Meditationes Vitate Christi*. M. Jordan-Stallings proves (against C. Fisher: *Die Meditationes Vitae Christi* [...] AFH, t. 25, 1932) the unity of the *Medit. Vitae* with the *Medit. Passionis*. These could have been written for Joan of Cattini, the Abbess of the Clarisses at San Giminiano. (See D. S. art. Jean "de Caulibus").

3. Jean Sonet *Répertoire d'incipit de prières en ancien français*, Genève, (Droz) 1956, p. 286, No. 1695.

4. Jean Sonet was not aware of the existence of the Boston Manuscript. See "Description des manuscrits" p.33.

5. *Devotissimum opus passionis Christi Meditationum incipit: a seraphico doctore Bonaventura editum, omnibus predicatoribus devotisque religiosis necessarium nun perrime impressum* [Venetiis per Petrum de Quarengiis Bergomensem. Anno M.cccc. XII. Die XX Kal. Martii.] Meditanda diebus Veneris & Sabbati: Incipiunt Mysteria Passionis Domini Jesu Cristi. fol. 35. *et seq.*

6. For instance in Ps.-Bonaventure, *op. cit.* fol. 37 v2; Ludolph of Saxony, *Vita Christi* Venetis (apud Guerrero Fratres et Franciscum Zilletum), 1581, fol. 598A. He died in 1378.

7. See, for instance, 599B:
   "In sudore autem notatur fervor: in sanguine,
   precium: in decursa, abundatia: in guttis,
   particularis efficacia, quamvis esset universalis
   sufficentia."

8. Same title as previously, but published: Pisauri per Petrum Capha in domo Ieronymi Soucini. Anno Domini M.D.X. Our text is, in fact, much more indebted to this version than any other and all subsequent references will be taken from it.

9. It is Abbé Georges Duriez's masterly *La Théologie dans le drame religieux en Allemagne au moyen âge* (Lille, 1914: in Mémoires et Travaux publiés par les Professeurs des Facultés Catholiques de Lille) which drew my attention to the wide use made, by mediaeval commentators, of the liturgical text.

10. See Duriez, *op. cit.*, p. 375.

11. See Duriez *op. cit.*, pp. 376-7.

12. Matthew mentions Pilate sitting on the judgment seat (27,v.19) and so does John (19,v.13). Also, the commentators: Petrus Comestor, for instance in his *Historia Scholastica*, cap. 166: "Quod Pilatus hora quasi sexta sedit pro tribunali" (Migne, P.L. vol 198, col. 627) and Ps. John Chrysostom, among others (i. e. probably Eusebius Alexandrinus). Πιλᾶτος ἐκαθέζετο κρινῶν, (Migne, P.G. Vol. 62 Tome 11, col. 721). In this text only have I found that Caiaphas "ou siege s'assist".

13. Ps. Bede, Migne P. L. Vol. 94 col. 563.

14. Ps. Bede, *loc. cit.*

15. Ludolph of Saxony, *op. cit.*, col. 603B.

16. Troyes, Bibliothèque Municipale. Ms. 1041: Anonymous sermon for Good Friday: *Christus passus est pro nobis.*

17. Luke 23, v.2.

18. John 18, v.33-38.

19. See Cornelius a Lapide. *Comm. in Matt.* XXVII, 15. Antwerp ed. 1732. p. 520 col.1. As regards the white vestment, the most exhaustive studies are to be found in Josef-Frederik Hekelius: *Dissertatio historico-philologico-theologica de habitu regio, Christo in Passione a Judeis, in ignominiam, oblato*. Chemnitz 1675 also: C.L. Schlichterus: *Observatio de alba Christi veste ad Luc. XXVII v.2.* Bremen, 1732.

20. Ludolf of Saxony, *op. cit.*, p. 621 col.A.

21. i. e. Jerome (*Epist. ad Eust.*); Prudentius (*Dist*); Ps. Bede (*De locis sanctis*); Petrus Comestor (*Historia Scholastica*); Ps. Bonav. (*Medit.*); Ps. Anselm (*Dialog. B. M. et Anselm.*); Birget *Revel.*); for a detailed study of the theme, see Duriez, *op. cit.*, p. 399.

22. Fer. III post Dom. Quinq. ad Vesp. I.

23. St. Birget, *Les Révélations célestes et divines de Sainte Brigitte de Suède communément appellée la chère espouse, divisées en huit livres* [...] Lyon (Simon Rigaud), ?1647. Bk I, ch. 10 p. 12; also in similar terms, Bk IV, ch. 70.

24. St. Birget, *loc. sic.*

25. See for instance *Le Livre de la Passion* ed. G. Franck
    Paris (CFMA), 1930, lines 1209-11, p. 41:
    > Pour le haster fort le boutoient / Prez qu'a terre
    > ne l'abatoyent / Et le poignoient d'aguillons.

26. See Duriez *op. cit.*, p. 409.
27. See St. Birget . *Revelations* (*ed. cit.*IV, 10. p. 12.)

28. See Duriez *op. cit.*, p. 416.

29. St. Birget. *ed. cit.*, p. 12/13.

30. Ps. Bonaventure. *op. cit.* Pisauri 1600 ed. fol. 67r.

31. *Meditationes devotissimae totius vitae D.N.J.C. secundum S. Bonaventuram* [....] Lugduni, apud A. Gryphium 1587, fol. 591.

32. Ludolf of Saxony, *ed. cit.* p. 639 col. B.

33. Ps. Bede, *De Meditatione Passionis Christi per septem diei horas libellus.* Migne P.L. vol. 94. col. 566.

34. Ps. Anselm, *Dialogus Beatae Mariae et Anselmi de Passione Domini.* Migne, P.L. vol. 159 (II) col. 282.

35. *Le Livre de la Passion*, lines 1353-7, p. 45.

36. *Sublime*: the cross was first erected then Jesus mounted it to be crucified.

37. *Humi*: Jesus was attached to the cross lying on the ground, then raised with it afterwards.

38. See chapter 5.

39. See Duriez, *op. cit.*, p. 419 - 420.

40. Although the miniature for Sext in the Boston Ms. shows a soldier brandishing three nails and the miniature for None shows Jesus on the cross, both feet nailed with one nail.

41. Ps. Anselm, *op. cit.*, ch. 10, col. 283.

42. *Loc. cit.*

43. Ps. Bonaventure, *ed. cit.*, fol. 70r.

44. Ludolf of Saxony, *ed. cit.*, p. 641, col. A.

45. Ps. Bede, *op. cit.*, col. 566.

46. See, for instance, Ps. Anselm: "Sitio" - "Quid, Domine, sitis?" - "Salutem peccatorum" *op. cit.* cap XII, col. 284.

47. That is, following the number of Paters recommended for each Canonical Hour by the Franciscan rule for lay brothers (see discussion of this point pp. 100)

48. *Evangelia Apocrypha*, G. Tischendorf ed. Leipzig, 1853. ch. VIII (XIV) p. 407. The name "Gospel of Nicodemus" does not appear until the XIIIth century. The more complete rendering of the Passion (The Acts of Pilate) is found in the 2nd Greek form only.

49. Ludolf of Saxony, *op. cit.*, p. 680, col. A.

50. Ps. Chrysostom, *op. cit.*, col. 724.

51. Ps. Anselm, *op. cit.*, cap. XV;, col. 286.

52. Charles Joseph Hefele, *Histoire des Conciles* Paris (Letouzey), 1916, Tome VII, part l. p. 608:
"11. Pour protester contre les hussites qui brûlent les images de Jésus crucifié et de la Sainte Vierge etc., on célébrera chaque année, le vendredi après le dimanche de *Jubilate* (troisième après Pâques) la fête des angoisses et des douleurs de Marie."
[Provincial council celebrated on March 20, 1423, at Cologne by the Cologne Archbishop, Thierry Dietrich II, Earl of Mörs. On April 22, 1423, the archbishop added a supplement of 5 canons to the 7 initial statutes. This is number 11.]

53. Ps. Anselm, *op. cit.*, cap. X, col. 283.

54. E. Mâle, *L'art religieux de la fin du moyen âge en France*. Paris (A. Colin), 1925, p. 126.

55. Ps. Anselm. *op. cit.*, cols. 286/287.

56. See Ludolf of Saxony, *op. cit.*, p. 668 col. A.

57. Ps. Bonaventure, *op. cit.*, fol. 89v.

58. *Ibid.*, fol. 91r. The same images are also found in Birget's *Revelations* (VII, 15).

59. See also: Matt. 27,v.45 and Mark 15,v.33.

60. See Dionysius Areopagite. Migne. P.G. vol. III col. 1081 (in Greek) and 1082 (in Latin) with Commentary by Balthasar Cordier, col. 1084.

61. J. de Voragine, *Legenda Aurea*. Art. S. Dionysius in all editions.

62. The gospel of Nicodemus; Petrus Comestor's *Historia Scholastica*; Anslem of Laon's *Glossa Ordinaria*.

63. Ludolf of Saxony, *op. cit.*, p. 661 col. B.

64. *Ibid*, p. 662 col. B.

65. Matt. 27, v.59-60; Mark 15, v.46; Luke 23, v.53.

66. Jo. 19, v.39-42.

67. See art. "Dévotion moderne": in *Dictionnaire de Spiritualité* [...] by Pierre Debongnie.

LITURGICAL USE

After the initial impact made by the strength and beauty of this Passion, one turns to wonder about the strange form of the poem. At first it appears unwieldy: 80 stanzas in a metre[1] very unusual in its brevity: each stanza having six lines and being, remarkably enough, a self-contained unit. The continuity of thought and sentiment in the author is such that this form does not detract from the unfolding of the *Passion* narrative, but it is there nonetheless.

An inner structure is indicated, though, in all three manuscripts, insofar as the Paris and Chantilly Mss give marginal indications to the Canonical Hours (A Matines; A Prime; A Tierce etc.,) and the Boston manuscript displays a miniature, depicting scenes traditionally connected with these Hours when relating to the *Passion*, at exactly the same position as do both French manuscripts. But looking at these scribal or iconographic indications the reader has, at least initially, all the more reason to be puzzled.

Of the 80 stanzas, two at the beginning and two at the end obviously serve as introduction and conclusion, though they are not included in the scheme proper to the Canonical Hours. This is very clear for the Introduction, since both the Paris and Chantilly Manuscripts give the indication *A Matines* after the first two stanzas.[2] As regards the two concluding stanzas they are not indicated as such or separated in any way from the "canonical" stanzas but their tone is such as to leave no doubt as to their rôle:

Ci finent ces diz / Extrais et hors pris...(st. 79)

We are thus left with the following structure:

2 (Introduction); 76 (Canonical Hours): 2 (Conclusion).

And the 76 stanzas for Canonical Hours are divided thus:

Matins	:	24	stanzas
Lauds	:	5	"
Prime	:	7	"
Terce	:	7	"
Sext	:	7	"
None	:	7	"
Vespers	:	12	"
Compline	:	7	"

My first thought was to make a connexion with the Roman Breviary according to the number of Psalms, i.e.: 3 x 3 (Matins); 5 (Lauds); 3 (Little Hours) etc., but this proved to have been a wrong track.

I owe it to Father J.G. Bougerol O.F.M. to have resolved my dilemma: he directed me to the Second Rule of Saint Francis, in the third chapter:

> Of the Divine Office and of Fasting, and How the Brethern should conduct themselves in the World:
> The Clerics must celebrate the Divine Office according to the order of the Holy Roman Church, except for the Psalter, for which they may use Breviaries. The Lay Brothers will recite twenty-four Pater for Mattins, 5 for Lauds, 7 for each of the Little Hours: Prime, Terce, Sext, None; twelve for Vespers and 7 for Compline. They will not forget the prayers for the Dead.[3]

This "Office of the *Paters*" seems to have been current practice and similar prescriptions are found in the rules of other religious Orders and it also applied to communities of women. Thus we read in the *Rewle of Sustris Minouresses enclosid*:

> Þe sustres whoche canne rede & singe schal do þe office reuerentli & mesurabli after þe custome & þe ordre of freris menoures, & þe oþer schal sey xx *Pater noster* | for matyns, v for laudis; For prime, tierce, sexte, none & complin, For eche owre vii *Pater noster*, And for euynsonge, xii *Pater noster* And in þis same maner be alle þinges in þe office of oure blissid ladi; be hit kepte wiþ deuowte preyinge for þe dede.[4]

The Third Order is subject to the same requirements both as far as clerics and *illiterati* (those who cannot read) are concerned. The latter recite twelve *Paters* for Matins and seven for each of the other Canonical Hours[5] together with *Gloria Patri*, the Creed and the *Miserere*.

If somewhat more complicated, the Rule for the Augustinian *Conversi* is basically similar:

I

Eodem tempore, surgant Conversi, quo & alii Fratres; & eodem modo inclinent. Cum surrexerint ad Matutinas, dicant Pater noster, & Credo in Deum: quod faciendum est ante Primam, & post Completorium. In Matutinis dicto Pater noster, & Credo in Deum, erigant se dicendo: Domine labia mea aperies &c. Pro Matutinis in profestis diebus dicant vigintiocto Pater noster,& in fine tantummodo dicant: Kyrie eleison. Pater noster &c. quo adicto dicant: per Dominum nostrum &c. dicendo: Benedicamus Domino etc. In Vesperis vero quatuordecim Pater noster, in aliis horis septem Pater noster dicant.

II

In Festis autem novem lectionum in Matutinis quadraginta Pater noster dicant; & hoc sub silentio in Ecclesia, vel ubicumque fuerint. Loco Pretiosa, tria Pater noster dicant. Pro benedictione mensae, Pater noster, Gloria Patri, &c. Post mensam pro gratiis, tria Pater noster, Gloria Patri, &c. vel Miserere mei Deus, qui sciunt.[6]

Regarding the Benedictines, Fr. Lowrie J. Daly S. J. notes, *à-propos* the *conversi*:

Their life was an austere, rugged life of hard manual labor conducted entirely in silence; their day began with a visit to the church and ended with the same, and they had the short simple prayers of the *Pater Noster* and *Gloria* for the canonical hours.[7]

The Dominican Rule is most precise about the Office of the *Conversi*. I quote from "The office to be said by Lay-Sisters":

Let the Lay-Sisters say their Office in the church or elsewhere as follows: for Matins, *Pater* and *Ave*, 24 times; for Pretioisa, 3 times; for Vespers, 12 times; for the other Hours, 7 times, adding at the beginning of the Hours: *Pater, Credo, Domine, labia mea* ...(Thou O Lord wilt open my lips...), *Deus in adjutorium*...(O Lord make haste...), *Converte nos*...(Convert us...) and at the end: *Per Dominum nostrum*... (Through our Lord...), *Benedicamus*...(let us bless...), according to the use in the Divine Office. For grace before meals let them say once *Pater, Ave*, and *Gloria*, and for grace after meals *Pater* and *Ave* 3 times or the *Miserere*. They may say their Office in their own language. They are not however bound to their Office under pain of sin, but obliged only by the Constitutions.

Instead of their own Office, the Lay-Sisters may with permission of the Prioress say the Little Office of the Blessed Virgin.[8]

This is very similar to the Franciscan Rule as far as the pattern of number is concerned, but here, *Aves* have also to be recited and there is a special provision (three *Paters* and *Aves*) in lieu of the *Pretiosa* (Reading of the Martyrology).

In fact, in order to get a clearer idea of that Office, here it is, reconstructed in full:[9]

Paters & Aves

Matins
Pater & Credo
Domine labia mea aperies
Et os meum annuntiabit laudem tuam.
Deus in adjutorium meum intende
Domine ad adjuvandum me festina
Gloria Patri....etc. Alleluia *or* Laus tibi Domine...12 Paters *and* Aves

Lauds
Deus in adjutorium meum intende
Domine ad adjuvandum me festina
Gloria Patri....etc. Alleluia *or* Laus tibi Domine... 12 Paters *and* Aves
Kyrie eleison, Christe eleison, Kyrie eleison
Pater
Per Dominum nostrum Jesum Christum Filium tuum, qui tecum vivit et regnat in unitate Spiritus Sancti Deus per omnia saecula saeculorum. Amen.
Benedicamus Domino
Deo gratias
Pater

Pretiosa
3 Paters *and* Aves

Prime
Pater and Credo
Deus in adjutorium meum intende
Domine ad adjuvandum me festina
Gloria Patri...etc. Alleluia *or* Laus tibi Domine....
7 Paters *and* Aves

Kyrie eleison, Christe eleison, Kyrie eleison
Pater
Per Dominum nostrum Jesum Christum Filium tuum, qui tecum vivit et regnat in unitate Spiritus Sancti Deus per omnia saecula saeculorum. Amen.
Benedicamus Domino
Deo gratias
Pater

Terce, Sext & None
Same as Prime except no Credo at beginning; Pater only

Vespers
Pater
Deus in adjutorium meum intende
Domine ad adjuvandum me festina
Gloria Patri...etc. Alleluia *or* Laus tibi Domine...
12 Paters *and* Aves
Kyrie eleison, Christe eleison, Kyrie eleison
Pater
Per Dominum nostrum Jesum Christum Filium tuum, qui tecum vivit et regnat in unitate Spiritus Sancti Deus per omnia saecula saeculorum. Amen.
Benedicamus Domino
Deo gratias
Pater

Compline
Converte nos Deus salutaris noster
Et averte iram tuam a nobis
Deus in adjutorium meum intende
Domine ad adjuvandum me festina
Gloria Patri...etc. Alleluia *or* Laus tibi Domine...
7 Paters *and* Aves
Kyrie eleison, Christe eleison, Kyrie eleison
Pater
Per Dominum nostrum Jesum Christum Filium tuum, qui tecum vivit et regnat in unitate Spiritus Sancti Deus per omnia saecula saeculorum. Amen.
Benedicamus Domino
Deo gratias
Pater *and* Credo

This, in fact, is the proof that the "Office of the *Paters*" had a definite canonical structure with the usual versicles and responses known by everyone, even the *illiterati*. The Franciscan Rule makes it quite clear that each Hour was to end with the Prayers for the Dead; either the *Fidelium animae per misericordiam Dei requiescant in pace. Amen* of the Roman Breviary, or a monastic equivalent:

> Et animae omnium fidelium defunctorum, parentum, fratrum, sororum, amicorum, benefactorum et malefactorum nostrorum per amarissiman passionem tuam intercessionem beatae Mariae Virginis ac Matris tuae et per merita omnium sanctorum requiescant in pace. Amen.

How is our Passion narrative connected to the preceding exposition? If we cast a glance again at the various Religious rules, we notice that the "Office of the *Paters*" in all of them and in the various versions are very similarly constructed. Yet only in the Second Rule of St. Francis is the pattern of numbers exactly similar to that of our *Passion*. Moreover, the approach of this narrative to the events of the Passion with its strong emphasis on the suffering of Jesus, a narrative devoid of any theological interpretation but appealing strongly to the heart of simple devout people, is more in the line of Franciscan spirituality than of any other monastic trend of the time. It appears that this Passion was written, most probably by a Franciscan and for Franciscans. But the question now arises: considering the structure of the poem, was this written with the "Office of the *Paters*" in mind, with no liturgical intention or, on the contrary, was it written for a definite liturgical occasion, and in order to fit the said "Office of the *Paters*"?

To answer this question we must turn to the actual recitation of that Office. W. de Paris writes:

> Tous les auteurs reconnaissent valeur canonique à cet "Office des Pater" et donc aussi les obligations canoniques d'un office liturgique de caractère public, même récité en privé.[10]

The Rule of 1223, which is still in use at present, underlines the obligation to all professed monks, *sub gravi* to recite this Office.

That this recitation was effected very much in the manner used by Choir Monks, is testified by this Act of the Constitutions:

> Nostri laici licite possunt, et valide recitare alternatim inter se ad modum chori officium proprium a Regula praescriptum, videlicet Orationem Dominicalem, etc.,[...] et ita successive dividere, ut unus primam partem dicat, et alter alteram".[11]

It appears from this that the recitation of the "Office of *Paters*" could be as solemn as that of the Office for choir-monks.

Let us at this point return to our text. We have noticed that the Canonical Hours are indicated by the rubrics: A Matines, A Laudes, A Prime, etc....If the text had been meant to be a meditation for each Hour, surely the author would have freed himself from the contingencies of such an unusual metre, and from the rather unwieldy numbers of stanzas. Let us also remember that the events described in the narrative correspond exactly to the sequence of the Passion, extending from the night of Thursday to Friday, until sunset on Friday. As a matter of fact, these divisions are those adopted by all writers on the Passion whenever they happen to divide their text according to Canonical Hours (Ludolf of Saxony, for instance, or the Venerable Bede). Is it not possible then, that, on Good Friday, when the Community would be devoting more time to prayer and meditation, the laybrothers or sisters for whom this poem had been composed would alternate each Pater with a stanza from the Poem, taking the place of a short meditation, thus maintaining in the mind the unfolding of the Passion?

This special devotion to the Passion is well in line with Franciscan spirituality. The Franciscans did a great deal to promote the devotion known as the *Stations of the Cross*, even if they did not establish it. This devotion practised in the Western Church throughout Lent (and even at other times during the year) is adhered to particularly during Holy Week and especially on Good Friday when it often follows the special Liturgy for that day. Wheras the Roman Church follows a standard procedure for this devotion, as clergy (and sometimes laity) proceed from one station to the next, including Versicles and Responses, orisons and hymns, other forms of this devotion are known to have been practised.

I came quite by accident on a published example of such an instance, parts of which bear such a strong resemblance with our text, that I consider it worthwhile to present it here at some length, all the more so as I believe this publication to be well-nigh unobtainable outside the Research Library at the University of California, Los Angeles. This is in an in-12 volume of 142 pages entitled *Via Sacra seu exercitum viae crucis dolorosae* [...] published in Turnow in 1763. It was composed by a Minorite priest and is

ad usum F. F. Min. ordinis Seraphici Reform. Provinciae S. Mariae Hungariae...

It gives 4 different ways of conducting the services; these are fairly similar to each other, it must be admitted, their main difference lying rather in the length and number of prayers, versicles and responses used at each station. Yet, one element is constant in all four: a *cantilena* in 18 stanzas is used while proceeding from one station to the next.[12]

The rubrics direct: "cantetur ex consueta Cantilena primus versus...". Thus it appears that, whereas the service was composed and assembled by the anonymous monk, the *cantilena* was already well-known (*consueta*). As good fortune has it, the music for the *cantilena* is given, in square notation, together with the first verse. It appears to be of XVIth century origin.[13] Here it is, transcribed in modern notation:

Passionem Domini recolamus pariter.
Fletu incessabili, omnes unanimiter.
In vocibus flebilibus, gemitibus, inenarrabilibus.

To sum up, we have here, purely and simply, a *cantilena* on the Passion of Christ, used as an integral part of a service. This one is in Latin; ours is in French.

What exactly is a *cantilena*? Amédée Gastoué has made a special study of this genre in two of his works.[15] Distinguishing between *cantilena romana* and *cantilena vulgaris* in the High Middle Ages, he writes:

> "Le terme de *cantilena* désigne, ou parait désigner, dans la forme latine du haut moyen âge, les formes de chant traditionnelles. La *cantilena romana*, c'est la mélodie liturgique qui suit le rit romain, organisé par Grégoire-le-Grand; une *cantilena vulgaris*, c'est un chant transmis de bouche en bouche, parmi le peuple, et ordinairement dans un langage non latin.[16]

and further defining the *farce*, together with its relationship with the *cantilena* he adds:

> [...]à partir du XIe s. [...]le chant en langue vulgaire, déjà introduit dans l'église, va prendre place dans l'office même, par le moyen de l'*épitre farcie* [....]Les épitres sont farcies soit en latin, soit en langue vulgaire. Quand la farce est en latin, elle

> paraphrase ou commente le texte, et sa mélodie est étroitement apparentée aux chants liturgiques.
> Lorsque, au contraire, la farce [...] est écrite en langue vulgaire, alors ces gloses sont toujours composées de strophes écrites sur le type de la cantilène, quant aux paroles; leur mélodie, quand elles en ont une de particulière, si elle a quelque rapport avec les airs de la liturgie, a bien plutôt une individualité très caractéristique, et plus proche des mélodies des cantilènes que nous pouvons connaître par ailleurs. Les exemples sont typiques: la forme mélodique, la disposition des groupes sur les syllabes, ne sont point celles des oeuvres liturgiques, mais bien celles des pièces écrites plus tard par les trouvères ou les troubadours."[...]
> Des farces en langue vulgaire ne sont point autre chose que des couplets de cantilènes, interpolant le texte sacré.
> "Il est [...] impossible de séparer l'une de l'autre l'histoire des cantilènes et celle des épitres farcies en langue vulgaire: l'un et l'autre genre demeurent, en même temps, la grande source du cantique français à l'église.[17]

Appraising the *cantilena* musically he writes:

> Musicalement, la cantilène est une mélodie bien constituée et proportionnée, de trois ou quatre membres bien déterminés. Tantôt - et c'est le cas le plus fréquent - sans refrain, tantôt avec refrain, ses strophes suivent toutes la même mélodie. En somme, en réduisant cette construction en formule on pourrait dire: dans la cantilène la mélodie change à chaque vers, mais elle reste semblable dans toutes les strophes. Dans le lai primitif, au contraire, la mélodie change à chaque strophe, mais elle est semblable dans tous les vers, quelque nombre qu'il en ait.[18]

I have chosen to give these lengthy quotations because Gastoué is and remains the specialist on, and main exponent of, *cantique populaire* (i.e. vernacular song in liturgy), and because these quotations provide an answer to the numerous questions I asked myself regarding this *Passion* and its actual liturgical usage.

Thus we learn that when the *farce* is in the vernacular, the glosses are in stanzas of the type of the *cantilena*. A *cantilena* is well structured into three or four clearly defined parts. Our text is indeed a gloss on the Passion composed in stanzas of a clearly defined pattern: two tercets rhyming *aab / aab*.

We also learn that, usually, the *cantilena* has no refrain, and this is also the case in our *Passion*.

Now, as regards the melody proper, for which we have no indication whatsoever in any of the *Passion's* three manuscripts, we learn that:
1. the melody changes with each line;
2. it remains similar within all the stanzas;
3. although the melody may have some connexion with liturgical airs, it is rather, in its form, that to be found in pieces composed by *troubadours* and *trouvères*.

The melody for the *Via Sacra* hymn transcribed above shows that lines 1 and 2 have the same melody but, apart from this, it falls in with the other criteria.

If we cannot speculate on the melody used in conjunction with our text, we can at least say that it corresponds to the form of the *cantilena*.

That the *cantilena* was sung on popular airs is affirmed by Gastoué[19] and is proved by the fact that Olivier Maillard composed a *chanson piteuse* in 1502, which he sung at Toulouse, during the service, using the melody "Bergeronnette Savoisienne".[20]

Whereas A. Gastoué distinguishes between *cantilena* (*romana* and *vulgaris*) and farce in the vernacular, M. Bukofzer distinguishes between *carol* and *cantilena*. He writes:

> The carol and its Latin counterpart, the Cantilena, do not differ in form. As a rule, an invariable burden leads off and then consistently alternates with an undetermined number of uniform stanzas or strophes. Since burden and stanza have different music, two strains alternate in performance.[21]

and further on, he adds:

> The general structure is the same in both forms: they both fall into burden and stanzas, which may differ in metrical structure and music, they both have the regular repeat of the burden after each stanza and the uniform pattern of the stanza itself, and they are both performed antiphonally or, strictly speaking, responsorially, in alternation between chorus and solo. The cantilena would indeed be identical with the processional hymn were it not for the difference in liturgical function, subject matter, metrical simplicity, and spirit which proves the important role of secular antecedents to the form.[22]

This clear definition reinforces strongly the suggestion I made above regarding the integration of the *Passion* poem in the "Office of the *Paters*":

the "invariable burden" being the *Pater*, alternating with the stanzas. Their metrical structure is, of course, very different and, musically, the *Pater* could be chanted by the whole community, either *mono tone* or on the melody used at Mass or on some other melody, whilst the stanza was sung on a melody probably well-known at the time, either by one monk or by several singing in unison.

That no record of the music is given in any of the three Passion Mss is not surprising. Refering to three carol collections, R. H. Robbins writes:

> The music which does not appear in any of the early preachers' books or in the special minstrel collections on account of lack of space, is nevertheless shown to be an essential part of the type by the three carol collections, all of which possess musical settings. [23]

The author of the "Passion Music" in Grove's Dictionary refering to the shorter text of the *Carmina Burana* (Munich Staatbibl. Ms. Latin 4660) which is given without music makes the same remark: "this is an omission of the scribe, for the words of the actors were undoubtedly sung".[24]

We must now ask ourselves how common was the practice of introducing an extraneous element in services. R. L. Greene affirms that the *cantilenae* "were, strictly speaking, extraliturgical, but they were produced under the auspices of the Church and were frequently introduced into services, particularly on feast-days",[25] and the XIVth century book of Ossory which contains Latin songs with vernacular verses gives the following pointer: "Episcopus Ossoriensis fecit istas cantilenas [...], ad cantandum in magnis festis et solatiis..." [26] Frank Ll. Harrison even notes that as early as the XIVth century, "polyphonic substitutes" were used for the *Benedicamus* at Vespers and were "also specifically allowed in the body of the Ordinal at Lauds and Vespers on Easter Day and at First Vespers on Trinity Sunday."[27] Such accretions to the liturgy were therefore readily accepted and our *Passion* finds its place easily within that framework. In his study of *Early English Carols*, R. L. Greene shows with superb clarity the influence of the Franciscans on the development of the carol which was "popular by destination" more than by origin and refering to the monk, mentioned in the Limburg Chronicle, who made songs, he quotes: "was er sang, das sangen die Leute alle gern...."[28] Although destined for monastic rather than for parochial use, our *Passion* fits with these remarks: The "Office of the *Paters*" was for use by *illiterati* or lay brothers.

We have already noted how well the tenor of our *Passion* fits with the Franciscan spirituality. Indeed, referring to Franciscan poetic composition, Greene remarks:

> Apart from this external evidence of the friars' activity in the realm of popular religious poetry to which the carol belongs, there are signs of strong Franciscan influence on the subject-matter and spirit of the carols. The tempering of the austerity of Christianity by the appeal to tender emotion and personal love for Christ, the invocation of pity for His sorrow in the cradle and suffering on the cross, which is particularly to be noted in the lullaby and Crucifixion carols, are part of the legacy of Francis to the centuries which followed his ministry.[29]

Our *Passion* is certainly in the line of Franciscan poetic activity of the time.

But wheras *carols* and *cantilenae* are usually compostions rather shorter than our text, it is worthwhile seeing whether larger compositions can be compared in scope and intention. We have already mentioned and examined the Turnow *Via Sacra*. I have chosen three more examples which will serve to illustrate the point and which, in effect, give support to my claims as to the use of the *Passion* under consideration. The first example is a very similar spiritual endeavour in a para-liturgical context, although from a different - but contemporary - monastic tradition: the service is recorded in the Dominican *Processionarium*. The second case is an actual Passion service entitled: *Cursus Sancte Bonaventure de Passione Domini* divided into Canonical Hours, and published in Vratislava in 1522. The third is taken from the Ligurgy of the Franciscans of Jerusalem published in 1623.

The Dominican service is called *Canticum de Passione Domini*. The devotion was initiated at the request of a Dominican nun, Catherine de' Ricci who had ecstatic visions of the Passion weekly between 1542 and 1554. St. Catherine told her confessor, Fra Timoteo, that Our Lady had taught her the Canticle immediately after her first experience, and he wrote it down. The canticle is in two parts: the first part is a succint narrative of the Passion made up of biblical quotations from the Psalms (21, 37, 43, 68, and 87); Isaiah ch. 50; Matt. ch. 27; Luke chs. 22, 23 and John ch.19. The second part is a meditation on the Passion made up in the same manner (Ps. 43 & 88; Isaiah ch. 12 and 53 and one verse from the *Te Deum*). A short time for meditation is allowed after each verse. Then follow a versicle, response and orison and the service ends with the Veneration of the Cross while the *Vexilla Regis* is sung. This devotion was immediately popular and received official recognition in 1644 when the Capitular Fathers meeting in Rome urged all Houses to practice this devotion regularly [30]. The melody used is extremely simple, witness this example for the first part of the services (note that it is very close to the Second Tone for the psalms: Intonation, Tenor and Flex, and Ending; only the Mediant is absent):

Amici mei et próximi mei *   advérsum me appropinquavérunt et stetérunt

Although this canticle is not meant to be integrated into an already existing service, as is the case for our *Passion*, nonetheless the spiritual content is very similar in both cases: narrative of the Passion and meditation on its purpose and the profit to be drawn from it for our redemption. The devotion is made into a service and chanted and this was undoubtedly the case for our *Passion*.

The second example is of much larger proportions. Its full title is: "*Cursus Sancti Bonaventure de passione Domini cum invitatoriis hymnis et canticis Laurencii Corvini: cum epistola et Carmine de gratuita Dei in nos beneficentia: et de fructibus ex dominice Passionis Recordatione provenientibus denuo Emendatus.* Impressum Vratislavie per Adam Dyonn Anno Domini 1522." Very little is known of Laurentius Corvinus. His biographer [32] tells us that he was born around 1465 at Neumark in Silesia. In 1488, he taught as Magister in the University of Cracow. He knew Conrad Celtis. He then went to Breslau and, after a short spell in Thorn, he returned to Breslau where he became aware of the incipient Reformation movement. He died on 21 July 1527. He wrote a number of Latin poems: *De Apolline et novem musis*; *Epicedium in Alexandrum Poloniae Regem* and others. He also wrote on Latin prosody: *Latinum Idioma*; *Hortulum elegantiarum*; *Compendiosa carminum structura*; *Delitiae Poetarum* etc...Also a *Cosmographia dans manducationem in tabulas Ptolemaei*. Nowhere have I been able to find any suggestions that he was linked with the Franciscan order. Corvinus gives a lengthy introduction to the service. It is full of classical references. On fol. 5v, he explains his aim thus:

> [...] in tam pietissimi muneris recordatione sepenumero psallendo recensuerimus que per sanctum Bonaventuram religionis nostre lumen et patrem clarissimum in perbrevem redacta sunt libellum cui ipse aliqua et quidem perpauca Hymnos etiam veros et cantica ex Saphicis Pindaricis et Iambicis carminibus addidi quos hymnos et psalmos perbreves si quis piam in tenero surgentis etatis flore aut dum grandior natu factus fuerit in redemptoris sui compassionem protulerit. (*sic.* for the whole passage).

Although he calls S. Bonaventure: *religionis nostre lumen et pater clarissimum*, this can hardly be a claim to his belonging to the Franciscan order. He admits to having composed the hymns based on Sapphic, Pindaric and Iambic models. It does not state that he composed the music. He explains that he divided the *cursus* into the seven canonical Hours (fol. 8v-9r.) but, in fact he separated Lauds from Matins, thus ending with 8 Hours.

Matins is preceded by the versicle and response V. Adoramus te Christe.... R. Quia per sanctam...and a *lectio brevis*: "Gratias ago tibi Domine [....] Dignare me laudare te benignissime Jesu Christe et sacratissime passioni tue laudes decantare". Then Matins proper begins with the usual versicles and responses and the following *Invitatorium*: "Christum Iesum inter maleficos pro nobis servandis crucifixum."

Then follow three short passages relating to the Passion of Jesus during the night, probably in lieu of Lessons. The *invitatorium* is repeated between each. Then comes the *Venite adoremus* followed by a short meditation; the *invitatorium*; *Gloria Patri*; *Venite adoremus* and the *invitatorium* again.

This is followed by a seven-stanza hymn, the last stanza being in the doxology form. Music is given for the tenor part.

The next part of Matins consists again of four short passages, this time drawn from the Scriptures, each ending with versicles and response, with the addition after the first passage of *Kyrie...Christe...Kyrie*; *Pater noster ...et ne nos* and *Jube domine*.

Matins ends with a *canticum pindaricum loco Te Deum Laudamus* which is not divided into stanzas. The music for descant and tenor parts is given, and the canticle is as usual followed by versicle and response.

It would be tedious and, indeed, going beyond the aim of this study, to give a detailed account of each Hour. Suffice it to say that the Office follows in its general lines the order of the Roman Breviary, and that, as announced, the *Invitatoria*, Canticles and Hymns, *Capitula* (sometimes) and orisons are "composed". I shall limit myself to listing here the forms adopted by Corvinius for Hymns and Canticles.

Matins	:	Hymn	: Hymnus Saphicus	Tenor
		(loco)Te Deum	: Canticum Pindaricum	Discantus/Tenor
Lauds	:	Hymn	: Hymnus Sapphicus	Discantus
Prime	:	Hymn	: Hymnus Iambicus	Discantus/Tenor
Terce	:	Hymn	: Hymnus Iambicus	Discantus/Tenor
Sext	:	Hymn	: Hymnus Iambicus	no music [33]
None	:	Hymn	: Hymnus Iambicus	Discantus/Tenor
Vespers	:	Hymn	: Hymnus Sapphicus	Discantus/Tenor[34]
Compline	:	Hymn	: Hymnus Iambicus	no music

After Compline various prayers follow, and a hymn "ad divam Catharinam" with music in four parts.[35] The publication ends with Erasmus' rules for the study of Holy Scripture.

Such a publication shows that, in 1522, one could engage the services of a humanist and a poet to produce a revised Good Friday service emcompassing all Canonical Hours, in the Franciscan tradition, (through the Bonaventurine *Meditations*), a tradition which, since the *poverello* had received the stigmata, had swept the whole of Western Christendom.

The third example is taken form the Franciscan liturgy: *Ordo Processionis* of the Franciscans of Jerusalem (church of the Holy Sepulchre) published in Venice, 1623 is the same as: *"Processiones quae fiunt quotidie a PP Franciscanis ad ss. Nascentis Christi Praesepe in Bethlehem: in Ecclesia*

Annuntiationis B. Virginis Mariae in Nazareth: *in Ecclesia ss. et Gloriosissimi Sepulchri Christi*: *in Ecclesia Salvatoris in Jerusalem*: [...] Antverpiae (ex officina Plantiniana Balthasaris Moreti M. DC. LXX." This also contains, in the same manner, a procession to the Crib at Bethlehem; one to Nazareth where Mary received the angel's message, and one to the place of the nativity of St. John the Baptist and the Visitation of Our Lady.

Pp. 31 - 54: Processio celebranda quotidie post Completorium Ierosolymis, per Ecclesiam sanctissimi et gloriosissimi Sepulchre Domini Nostri Iesu Christi.

The service is divided into thirteen parts each containing Hymn, Antiphon, Versicle and Response and orison - although part 1 (Before the Holy Sacrament) has no hymn - the sequence of the other twelve parts is as follows:

(2) Ad columnam flagellationis;
(3) Eundo ad carcerem;
(4) Ad locum divisionis vestimentorum Christi;
(5) Ad locum inventionis S. Crucis;
(6) Redeundo ad capellam S. Helenae
(7) Ad columnam coronationis et improperiorum;
(8) Quando processio ascendit ad montem Calvariae,pro loco crucifixionis;
(9) Ad locum ubi Crux cum Christo fuit erecta, atque collocata;
(10) Descendendo ad lapidem ubi Christus fuit inunctus;
(11) Pro glorisissimo Christi Domini Sepulchro;
(12) Ubi Christus apparuit Mariae Magdalenae in hortulani habitu;
(13) Tandem ad Capellam Virginis Mariae.

The first line of the tune of the hymn is given in each case, but not that of the antiphon, except in the case of the last antiphon (see below). The orison was also chanted since, in the case of the 9th station, the rubrics mention: "sed dicitur sine cantu".

After the hymn of the thirteenth station, the Litanies of the Virgin are recited and the Service ends with eleven orisons appearing elsewhere in the *Processionale*.

As an example of the music used, here is the chant for the last antiphon:

Gaude Virgo Mater Christi
Condemnatum quem vidisti
Resurrexit, sicut dixit.

Gaude lumen claritatum:
Quem vidisti conclavatum,
Resurrexit, sicut dixit.

Gaude decus virginale:
Quem vidisti expirare,
Resurrexit, sicut dixit.

Gaude flos odoris miri:
Quem vidisti sepeliri,
Resurrexit, sicut dixit.

Gaude, gaude, Virgo Mater Christi:
Gloriosum quem vidisti
Resurrexit, sicut dixit.
Alleluia, Alleluia, Alleluia.

It is particularly sad that the superb liturgical collection of the British Museum (Shelf marks 3355; 3356; 3366 and 3395) was destroyed during the air raids on London. This unfortunately reduced the scope of research in Franciscan liturgies considerably.

Viewed in the light of the foregoing services, our *Passion* takes its place in a well-established tradition, both secular (in the sense of parochial) and monastic. I have shown that these compositions were not merely academic or artistic, separated from their original context but, on the contrary, that the Church was strong enough to integrate them into its liturgical pattern, on more solemn occasions.

To close this chapter, I shall attempt a hypothetical reconstruction of one of the Canonical Hours of this *Passion*, following the examples presented above. Bearing in mind that this would be for a public (not a private) recitation, [36] the order of Vespers would probably have been as follows:

                Pater (et Ave) *secreto*

Deus in adjutorium meum intende.
Domine, ad adjuvandum me festina.
Gloria Patri et Filio et Spiritui Sancto.
Sicut erat in principio, et nunc et semper,
et in saecula saeculorum. Amen.
Laus tibi Domine, Rex eterne gloriae.

    Pater...(intoned)
    Quand Jesus fina... [st. 60]   (known melody)

    Pater...(intoned)
    De ce Saint Denis... [st. 61]   same melody

    Pater...(intoned)
    O Vierge Marie... [st.62]   "

    Pater...(intoned)
    Tendrement plourant... [st. 63]   "

    Pater...(intoned)
    Gens plains de meschance.. [st.64] "

    Pater...(intoned)
    Quant sa lance ostoit.. [st.65]   "

    Pater...(intoned)
    Longin fut celui... [st.66]   "

    Pater...(intoned)
    Ses yeulx en frotta... [st.67]   "

    Pater...(intoned)
    Paine toy, labeure... [st.68]   "

    Pater...(intoned)
    Regarde comment... [st.69]   "

    Pater...(intoned)
    Ilz vont saluer... [st.70]   "

Pater...(intoned)
Celle Vierge douce... [st.71]   same melody

Kyrie eleison. Christe Eleison. Kyrie eleison.
Pater... *secreto*
Per Dominum nostrum Jesum Christum
sub silentio qui vivit et regnat...
Benedicamus Domino
Deo gratias
Fidelium animae per misericordiam
Dei requiecant in pace.
Amen.
Pater...*secreto*

NOTES

1. See chapter 3, p. 49.

2. As to the Boston Manuscript, its sheer physical lay-out makes this distinction impossible, the miniature being always placed at the top of a folio.

3. *Opuscules complets de St. François d'Assise* [...] par le traducteur des oeuvres de Catherine Emmerich. Tournai 1864. p. 102. This rule was approved by Pope Honorius. (Transl. by the present author).

4. *Two fifteenth-century Franciscan Rules*. Ed. Walter W. Seton London, (EETS), 1914, p.85.

5. See Gerald Joseph Reinmann J.C.L., *The Third Order of St. Francis*, Studies in Canon Law No. 50. Catholic Universtiy of America, Washington DC, 1928. See also Francesco Mattesini O.F.M., *Le Origini del Terz' Ordine Francescano*. Milano. n. d.

6. *Regula S. Augustini et Constitutiones FF. ordinis Praedicatorum*. Romae, 1690. Distinction Secunda. cap. XV (I and II) pp. 326-7.

7. Lowrie J. Daly, S.J. *Benedictine Monasticism*. New York, n.d.

8. *Constitutions of the Nuns of the Sacred Order of Preachers* [...] (Vatican Press), 1930. Part I, ch. XVI, art. 2, paras. 214 and 215.

9. I wish to express my thanks to Sister Mary-Pia, O. P., Mistress of Novices at the Monastery of Our Lady of Angels, Los Angeles, for her scholarly help in this and in the matter of the *Canticle of the Passion of the Lord* , discussed below.

10. Viller, *Dictionnaire de Spiritualité* [...] vol. V, col. 1213. Article "Frères Franciscains" by W. de Paris.

11. *Monumenta ad Constitutiones Ordinis Fratrum Minorum Capuccinorum pertinenta*. ed. Rmus P. Venantius-à-Lisle-en-Rigault. Romae (Curia Generalitia), 1916. ch. III, art. 49, p. 139.

12. There are sixteen (and not fourteen) stations in this devotion, and two stanzas are used before the beginning of the service.

13. I am indebted to Prof. Gilbert Reaney for this identification and for his willingness in discussing, and finally approving, the various theories put forward in this chapter.

14. The full text of the *Cantilena* is given in Appendix C.

15. Amédée Gastoué. *Variations sur la musique d'Eglise.* Paris (Schola), 1913; and: *Le Cantique populaire en France.* Lyon (Janin), 1924.
16. Amédée Gastoué. *Le Cantique*....p.6.
17. *Ibid.*, p. 18 - 20.
18. *Ibid.*, pp. 54 - 5.
19. See A. Gastoué. *Variations*....p. 20.
20. O. Maillard, *Chanson piteuse composée par frère Olivier Maillard en pleine prédication au son de la chanson nommée "Bergeronnette Savoisienne" et chantée à Toulouse environ la Penthecouste par ledit Maillard lui estant en chaire de prédication, l'an mil cinq cens et deux. Et bien tost apres trespassa.* s. l.?1502.
21. Manfred, F. Bukofzer, *Studies in Medieval and Renaissance Music.* London (Dent), 1951. P. 149.
22. *Ibid.*, pp. 149 - 150.
23. R. H. Robbins, "The earliest Carols and the Franciscans" in *Modern Language Notes* vol. 53, No. 4. April 1938. Pp. 244 - 5.
24. Grove's Dict. 5th ed. 1954, art. "Passion Music", p. 577, by Ch. Stanley Terry with revisions and and additions by William L. Smoldon.
25. R. L. Greene, *The Early English Carols.* Oxford (Clarendon), 1935, p. Lxxxviii.
26. R. H. Robbins, *art. cit.*, p. 240.
27. Frank Ll. Harrison, *Music in Medieval Britain.* London (Kegan Paul), 1958, p. 111. See also table facing that page.
28. R. L. Greene, *op. cit.*, pp. xciii, cxx.
29. *Ibid.*, p. lxxvii.
30. See William R. Bonniwell, O.P., *A History of the Dominican Liturgy.* New York (Joseph Wagner), 1944, pp. 316 - 7.
31. The complete form of this service is given in Appendix D.
32. *See Allgemeine deutsche Biographie.* Leipzig, 1876.
33. Since the form is similar to the Hymn for Terce, it is assumed that the music for Sext is similar to that noted for Terce. The same applies to Compline.

34. Music similar to Terce. In fact the music plate for Terce (fol. 17v) has been used integrally for None (fol. 20v.)

35. Both are reproduced in Appendix E., with the "Canticum Pindaricum Loco Te Deum" (fol. 13r. & v.) for Matins.

36. One more element which militates in favour of a public recitation is the fact that, in the Boston Ms. Matins and Lauds are not treated separately (Lauds begins simply with a more elaborately decorated initial) and it is a rule that, when recited publicly, in choir, Matins cannot be separated form Lauds: "In publica vero recitatione Matutinum in Choro a Laudibus separari non potest" (Rubrics of the Roman Breviary).

THE MINIATURES OF THE BOSTON MANUSCRIPT

Of the three manuscripts containing the Franciscan Passion, only one, the Boston P.L. 1551 = Med. 129, is decorated in any significant manner. The Chantilly 141 has decorated initials with pen flourishes and the Paris 190 has only five historiated letters.

It is tempting to say that the Boston Ms. is decorated sumptuously. This adverb can hardly apply to *grisaille*, but the overall impression created is so overwhelming in its stark desolation and dignity and indeed, so well-adapted to the subject of the Passion, that the viewer cannot but feel that he is in the presence of a great masterpiece.

There are seven miniatures, each introducing a Canonical Hour. They all measure 76/78mm X 60mm. The first one is integrated in a floral border which will be discussed below; it is on the *recto* of the folio, as are the next five miniatures. The seventh is on a *verso*.

The subjects of the miniatures are:

For Matins	:	The betrayal in the garden of Gethsemane and the healing of Malchus' ear	fol.1r.
For Prime	:	Jesus before Pilate	fol.9r.
For Terce	:	The scourging of Jesus	fol.11r.
For Sext	:	Jesus carrying his cross	fol.13r.
For None	:	Jesus dies on the cross	fol.15r.
For Vespers	:	The descent from the cross	fol.17r.
For Compline	:	The entombment	fol.20v.

I shall first give a brief overall description of each miniature without dwelling on its particular features. These latter (costumes, armaments, landscapes, technique, etc.) will be separately discussed. I shall study the features that identify and date the Ms; those that make it part of an artistic family; and those that make it unique.

1. *The Betrayal in the garden of Gethsemane and the healing of Malchus' ear.*

An enclosure marked out by a wooden palisade and a heavy double-gated doorway surmounted by a dovecote. One of the gates opens out onto the country with small hills undulating to the horizon. In the distance, on a rock where, shortly before, Jesus was praying to his Father: "O my Father, if thou be willing, remove this cup from me" (Luke 22, v.42), rests a chalice with a wafer above it. A golden ray from above falls onto them. The shimmering scene puts touches of light on the rock itself and the nearby tree and recalls, symbolically perhaps, the institution of the Eucharist which took place shortly before the time represented by this scene. In the enclosure is a compact group of armed soldiers, one of them carrying a lighted lantern (Jo. 18, v.3). Jesus is in the centre of the group; his face, dignified and peaceful, is radiant with light, touches of which are reflected by the arms and armour and on the planes of the faces of those surrounding him. On the left, and somewhat outside the group, Simon Peter, who has just struck Malchus, is seen with his sword raised above his head, and his left hand still holds the scabbard. The disciple is almost bald: a tuft of hair above his forehead and a bushy grey beard. His face expresses both sadness and wrath. A thin line of gold indicates his halo. The servant of the high-priest is a young man, almost a child. The force of the blow has thrown him to the ground. He still holds his lantern in his left hand, but it has gone out and lies on the ground beside him. With his right arm he still tries to protect himself from the blow and his childish face expresses astonishment and fear. His short, soft tunic dotted with gold at the collar, is embroidered in the middle of the chest with 2 letters: A and F, separated by an elongated knot. But already Jesus points his finger to Malchus' ear and heals him (see st. 20). Judas takes advantage of this episode to approach his master. His face is grey. He seems to hesitate, perhaps to regret, an action which is already irreversible. He looks at Jesus sideways and his arm is already half around Jesus' neck. Meanwhile a soldier drags Jesus' left hand and binds it. There is a striking contrast between the soldiers with savage, brutal faces pressing around their prisoner, tense and obviously anxious not to let him escape, and the peaceful, detached, countenance of Jesus whose youthful face and high forehead are surrounded by a cruciform halo.

2.   *Jesus before Pilate.*

Whereas the text follows closely enough the narrative of St. John, this second miniature takes its inspiration from St. Matthew since it represents Pilate washing his hands. The same soldiers who, the night before, arrested Jesus and took him before Annas and the Sanhedrin, now push him before Pilate. The painting does not represent Pilate's wife (Matt. 27, v.19) as is often done in the depiction of this episode of the Passion.

The hall of judgement is bare and cold. Thus all interest concentrates on the *personae*. On the left is the entrance to the hall (the perspective is very free) and one step of the threshold. The impression of perspective is created by the receding lines of the paving slabs and the beams of the ceiling. This would be quite convincing were it not for the canopy above the seat of judgment, whose pelmet goes against the established perspective.

Jesus is at the centre of the painting. He is surrounded by six soldiers whose arms and armour as well as facial expressions are clearly recognizable as those of the previous painting. The tense stance of the soldiers contrasts sharply with that of the prisoner: relaxed and detached, his hands slipped in the sleeves of his robe. Here, Jesus bears no trace of torture (this departs form the johannic tradition) but his face is drawn and his eyes are swollen and bear witness to a sleepless night. This time his head is not surrounded by a halo, but by cruciform golden rays. A strand of hair is stuck to his forehead. Jesus' face is impressive: his inward gaze is intense. The head is slightly bent towards the left shoulder and he looks with resignation at the basin in which Pilate is washing his hands.

It is Pilate who, in this painting, attracts and holds the attention. He is sitting in the seat of judgment, his bust slightly turned toward us. He is clad in a long robe over which he wears a metal breast-plate which reflects the light. On his head is a felt peaked cap with narrow rolled brim. His left hand is in the basin which sits uneasily on the arm of the chair. His other hand is in his lap. But the interest resides in its dramatic force: it is the face of a frightened weak man. His hair and beard are untidy and cannot hide the flabby cheeks and the mouth with drooping commissures. The psychological realism of the face and look is frightening. Here is a man who lacks the courage to look at the one he is condemning to death and he keeps his eyes level with the legs of the accused. Heavy circles under his eyes reinforce the impression of shameful defeat.

Here again all the light of the picture emanates from the face of Christ and is reflected on the helmets and armour of the soldiers and on Pilate, the pelmet and the wooden panels of the seat of judgment; and Pilate, being seated between Jesus and the tapestry falling at the back of his seat, projects his own shadow on the tapestry.

The strong dramatic interest of this painting resides in the psychological contrast between Jesus and Pilate.

3. *The scourging of Jesus.*

Here again there is no superfluous detail to allow the imagination to escape. The walls, ceiling and floor are blank and bring us inexorably to the display of suffering. In the foreground the column (the only one in the room) where Christ is bound has no architectural function: in the mind of the artist, its only function is that of a torture-post. Its round shaft is slender and polished, its base round, and the capital is vaguely gothic. Here again, the *décor* does not preoccupy the artist. The paving stones (halved in two tones of grey triangles) and the beams of the ceiling are similar to those of the preceding miniature. But whereas everything in that one was static, in this one everything is movement. Jesus is bound to the column at his wrists and ankles. The hands are crossed around the column and bound tightly, but the ankles are only loosely bound around it: a refinement of cruelty which compels the prisoner to find his balance after each lashing. This impression of movement is again accentuated by the sinuous shape of the cord binding the wrists of the victim and held at both extremities by the torturers.

As for Jesus, he is naked save for a loincloth. His left shoulder is leaning against the column and he bends his knees in order to keep his balance. The body is thin and the rib-cage stands out. The arms and the chest show long weals made by the lashings. The face now bears the marks of the suffering: it is soiled, streaked with sweat. Strands of hair are stuck to the wet forehead, the cheeks and the shoulders. And yet the face is in moving contrast with the marks of physical degradation. Christ's face remains peaceful, its expression rather inturned. It is still surrounded by cruciform rays which remain the same in all miniatures. The intense impression of movement and activity comes mainly from the two tormentors whose bodies, flexing synchronically (one towards us, the other away from us) as well as the cord that links them to their victim, indicate without doubt that they are turning around Jesus. The striking realism of movement is comparable to that of the pen drawings in the Munich Bible[1] by the Master of Catherine of Cleves.

The tormentor's face on the right expressess an intense and bestial hatred. The square jaw, profile and vicious small eyes are indeed so similar to those of one of the soldiers in the first miniature that it is difficult to avoid the thought that the artist took as his model a real person for whom he had little sympathy.

4. *Jesus carrying his Cross.*

The number of figures on the scene, their attire, the intense activity and movement, all recall the setting of the first miniature. Here again, the landscape is only roughly sketched, and so is the architecture. The artist concentrates essentially on the human drama. The cross (T-shaped) dominates the painting. The holes for the nails are already made. The artist had first drawn it smaller, with a ruler, but later prolonged one of the arms and the foot, this time without the help of a ruler, and the joins are neither straight nor accurate. The lengthening of the foot of the cross also means that it now extends beyond the lower frame of the picture. Jesus has just passed through the gate leading out of Jerusalem. It is a massive affair: we discern an enormous round pillar without any ornament, a low threshold beyond which one makes out some sort of vague paving and, above, at the upper limit of the frame, the *portcullis* which has been raised to allow the prisoner and his escort to go out. On the right and in the centre-ground, a roughly sketched hillock crowned with two trees. The same hillock will appear in the last two miniatures, but on the left, thus giving us an impression of progression towards the place of crucifixion. The line of the horizon is rather high and the sky is faintly touched with blue. The road is uneven and is strewn with large stones on which Jesus will soon stumble.

As in the first miniature, 9 soldiers close in around Jesus. He wears his robe gathered at the waist with a belt, in order to avoid unnecessary stumblings, as the weight of the cross bends him forward. Jesus balances the cross on his left shoulder and his face is turned toward us. He now wears the crown of thorns; his beard is caked with blood around the mouth. The eyelids are heavy with lack of sleep but the far-away detached look is comparable with that in the preceding miniatures. The lassitude, the collapsed state of the victim's body are heart-rending (see st. 48).

Counting the number of arms held high above the soldier's heads, six are compactly massed behind Jesus, while three more soldiers placed in front and behind and near him lend the picture a truly superb balance; and, in contrast with the first group, these three play a more active role in the scene, thus enhancing Jesus' predicament. One of them leads Jesus along like an animal. He has attached a cord to the prisoner's right wrist and holds it in a casual manner, flung across his right shoulder. We only have a back view of this soldier, but through his swaggering gait the artist allows us a masterly glimpse of the soldier's mental attitude and lends a startling realism to the scene. In his left hand he holds the three nails of the crucifixion.[2]

Immediately behind Jesus another soldier hits him in the small of the back with his knee; a cynical sneer pulls his face sideways. He carries a mace lightly balanced on his right shoulder and conveys the impression of longing to crash it on the condemned man's head. He grasps and pulls a handful of Jesus' hair with his left hand.

Two other soldiers have also a role in this scene: they are behind the cross, at Jesus' head and above him, as they are not bent down with the weight of the cross. The face of one of them is partially hidden by his colleague's helmet. He seems to weigh, without animosity, the strength of the victim and the small likelihood of his carrying the cross as far as the place of execution. The other soldier's face is turned toward Jesus and his eyes are partially hidden by the visor of his helmet. He displays the same feelings as his companion, but also a certain compassion. It would even seem that he is trying to alleviate the weight of the cross by lifting it with his shoulder.

All this scene is made up of human conflicts, and the contrasting of expressions and passions.

5.   *Jesus dies on the Cross.*

We are now on Mount Calvary. All is utterly still and silent, as after a great catastrophe. The sky and the earth are uniformly grey. A sinuous road strewn with large stones meanders between hillocks and ends near the towers of the city of Jerusalem in the background. But, as is always the case, the scenery has no importance in itself. In fact, the sketching is skimped: the hills are made of approximately rounded strokes; the grass is dealt with in summarily crossed brush strokes; and as to the trees, they are depicted by a simple circle and a hasty scrawl in the centre with a downward stroke for the trunk, their shadows being shown by means of a few approximate hatchings.

Jesus' cross dominates the picture. It is planted in the middle of the foreground and is, in fact, hardly contained within the limits of the frame. It now carries the superscription INRI on a small bevelled board. The body of Christ is stretched to the utmost. The tendons of the arms are bulging and the hands and feet gather up around the nails. The right side has been opened by the spear and a long brown streak runs down to the groin. The weight of the body bends the knees and from the wound of the feet issues a trickle of blood which stains the wood (see st. 54). The head of the crucified man is bowed towards the right and, in fact, the whole body slumps slightly to the right. The eyes are half-closed: Jesus has just died.

The Virgin and St. John are on either side of the cross. She is on his right: an older woman, heavy and hunched up, her face stiff with sorrow, gazing at the foot of the cross. She is wrapped from head to foot in a long veil that she keeps bunched up behind her joined hands, which are squeezed against her belt. On the other side, St. John, a very young man, keeps his face lifted up to Christ. He holds his cloak in the same way as the Virgin holds her veil. Both have a thin gold halo.

In the middle ground the thieves are crucified one on either side of Jesus, and their crosses show a good perspective. Their arms have been cruelly tied with ropes behind the horizontal bars of the crosses and the ropes brought down loosely around their legs. That they are not dead yet is evident from the way they thrash with their legs in an effort to relieve their agony. Their faces (and particularly that of the thief on the left) are contorted with suffering.

Thus the contrast between the horror of the thieves' deaths on the one hand, and that of Christ's quiet and dignified one on the other, is quite striking.

6.   *The descent from the Cross*

A first inspection could suggest that the artist responsible for the backgrounds had simply not taken the previous miniature into account. For Christ's cross is still at the very centre of the foreground, the crosses of the thieves have disappeared and so has Jerusalem (in the background), and the hillocks which appeared rather small in the previous miniature, seem closer and larger in this one and the next. This conclusion, however, turns out to be wrong and gives little credit to the integrity of the artist or to the coordination of work in the workshop. In fact, whereas, in the previous painting, the scene is viewed from some little distance, away from the cross, at the height, say, of a standing person, this miniature and the next are viewed not only more closely, but also as from the eye level of a person kneeling or squatting (as are the Virgin, St. John and Nicodemus); thus the landscape naturally appears foreshortened and somewhat distorted, and Jerusalem disappears behind the contours of the ground.

The composition is very impressive. An attendant standing on a ladder which leans on the cross has just detached the second arm of Jesus, the left one, and holds him at the wrist, whilst on the other side Joseph of Arimathaea looking lovingly at Jesus receives him in his arms and Mary, kneeling on one knee, holds the inert right arm of her son and kisses it, with her face lifted towards him. The feet of the crucified man are still nailed to the cross and Nicodemus with the help of huge pincers is trying to remove the nail. St. John is kneeling behind the Virgin, his hands are joined in an attitude of prayer; his face expressing intense sadness has unfortunately been marred, probably at a later date, by droplets of water.

The unity of the scene comes from the beautiful grouping of persons centering on Jesus' oblique stance, and also from the upturned faces of Joseph of Arimathaea, Mary and St. John, expressing love and compassion.

7.   *The entombment.*

Without recapitulating my remarks regarding the landscape in the previous miniature, I must observe that here, in the present painting, the eye of the beholder of the scene (the artist) is even lower still. It is at the height of the unction stone on which Jesus has been laid, and as this is in the foreground, the cross is now in the middle ground, with the ladder still resting against it.

As usual, the grouping of persons is masterly. Indeed, although it does not depart in any way from tradition, the angle of the unction stone, the attitude of each person, and the focusing of their gazes, make the scene compelling.

The angle at which the unction stone is placed corresponds to that at which the ladder is propped against the cross. The body of Christ appears to be already stiff (i. e. to have set in *rigor mortis*) and it has been laid on a shroud held at both extremities, as is traditional, by Joseph of Arimathaea and Nicodemus. One of them, at the feet of Christ still wears more or less the same attire as in the previous miniature, whereas the other appears to have exchanged his apparel for that of the traditional pilgrim: a vast robe with scalloped shoulders and a large hat with its front brim upturned and decorated with the scallop shell. (These details are discussed further down). The body of Christ has lost the luminosity which served to light up all the other miniatures: it has been painted with a very light ochre wash, giving it an ivory-like appearance, and the green crown of thorns is still around the head.

Behind the unction stone - shaped, according to the misconception of the period, like a sarcophagus (to be discussed later) - stands a compact group of six persons. The Virgin is kneeling by the stone. She has seized the right hand of her son and presses it against her cheek whilst, with her right hand, she caresses his forearm. She is slumped towards Jesus and looks at him with an air of utter sadness and resignation. She wears the same veil as in the two previous miniatures, maintained, it seems, by a coif: the effect is very reminiscent of the headdress of the Béguines. Next, and slightly behind her, stands John who holds her by the shoulders. His head is likewise inclined to the left and he looks at the body of Christ with an air of utter desolation. Behind him stand four (and not three) women in a dress similar to that of the Virgin, their stiff veils pulled well over their foreheads and their attitude is that traditional for mourners.

In this painting, and this one only, Christ is no longer at the centre of the picture. That position is occupied by the Virgin.

Iconographical Study

1. *Genre*

The Boston Manuscript miniatures are painted in *grisaille*. Earlier in this chapter, I spoke of a sumptuous decoration; to this one could add, without contradiction, that the *grisaille* is unrelieved, for indeed, in their austerity, the miniatures remain a testimony to the sombre yet regal majesty of Good Friday: the artists who contributed to the decoration of the manuscript were certainly fully conversant with the desolation as well as with the grandeur of the liturgy for that day. Molly Tysdale Smith thinks that: "the use of gray monochrome in church liturgical practices may have spread from the era in Northern France, chiefly in the School of Paris, where the *Altarcloth of Narbonne* and similar pieces were executed, to near-by Burgundy, where we find other inventory descriptions of the same types, and to Flanders. The use of *grisaille* in manuscript miniatures seems to have followed the same path."[3]

The first impression is that all miniatures are painted exclusively in various tones of grey. It is only on close examination that one can detect very faint traces of other colours. The grey itself gives an overall impression different from that in any other manuscript painted in *grisaille*. Here, lighter or darker, the tonality is slate grey. Whereas *grisaille* in town scenes by Le Tavernier as in the *Conquêtes de Charlemagne*, for instance, can be extremely bright, here, the cold blue colour added to the greys lends the pictures a feeling of utter sadness. The other colours used in the Boston manuscript and that, as I have said, very sparingly, are, with one exception, all cold colours. They are: terre-verte and burnt Sienna used for hair; gold ochre for faces; blue (lapis lazuli) for sky; these three recur in all miniatures. Russet-brown is used for the blood flowing from Christ's wounds in one painting, and green (probably arsenic and milk casein) for the crown of thorns in four miniatures. The use of gold is very restrained. It appears in all miniatures for haloes and, generally, to pick up very sparingly the light which emanates from Christ. Each miniature is in a frame of mauve and blue and the initials are in the same colours, in alternation. In the first miniature, the lantern held by one of the soldiers has a touch of orange and the sombre glow is quite effective.

The sober technique of the *grisaille* imparts to the miniatures a feeling, as L. Delaissé put it,[4] of "quiet sadness". One may indeed pinpoint the essential difference between the various types of *grisaille* found in French, Flemish or Netherlandish manuscripts on the one hand, and the Boston Passion on the other. In the former, *grisaille* is used mostly as a "device" to induce a feeling of solemnity, or to compel attention by suggesting an impression of "sculptures in stone colour,"[5] whereas, in the Boston manuscript, one feels that the miniatures could not have been painted differently; that this was the only possible way of representing the Passion; that, indeed, the garden of Olives looked exactly as it is painted here; that Jesus was scourged exactly as painted here. There is, in these miniatures, an impression of inevitability which makes them wholly compelling.

2. *Techniques of painting*

Looking closely at the miniatures, it appears that the background was prepared in all cases in a similar manner: probably with two coats of very weak gesso and an isolating coat, perhaps of skimmed milk. This background is still visible on the bottom right-hand and left-hand corners of the first miniature and along the bottom edge of the second one, where the person who applied the imprimature of grey gouache did not do it too carefully.

The drawing was mainly sketched in charcoal. Traces of charcoal are still visible in several places and mainly in the fourth miniature: "Jesus carrying the cross", where the lines indicating the masses have not been properly erased and where the horizontal beam of the cross shows no fewer than five charcoal lines, indicating various attempts at lengthening the left arm of the cross;[6] also the threshold of the gate on the left was first drawn somewhat lower than it finally appears. Similar remarks could be made about other miniatures.

The drawing was also, in certain cases, done with a metal point, perhaps a silver point. This is shown very clearly in the miniature of the "scourging", for instance, where the hood of the right-hand varlet was first drawn as a lowish triangular point but was finalised as a collar. The skin had been scratched there and the attempt made to cover the scratch with brush-strokes was unsuccessful. Yet the triangular design was not abandoned: it is found in the fifth miniature on St. John's robe, but this time it appears on the chest, not on the back.

We may next ask ourselves whether the artist - or artists - drew each figure, each group, completely freehand or used, more or less liberally, a set of patterns available to the workshop. I have compared the drawing of heads, feet, figures, weapons and trees in the seven miniatures and have drawn the following conclusions:

Two main types of faces are drawn repeatedly here, which could be called the "young head" (beardless) and the old head (with beard and headdress). Of the former, one can place in parallel the face of Judas and that of Malchus in the first miniature and the face of John in the fifth one. In all three cases the head leans at a similar angle on the left shoulder; the hair flows freely to the left and the shapes of the eyes, nose and mouth are quite similar. Yet, in the case of Judas and Malchus the expressions, as indicated in the first part of this chapter, are quite different (see illustration I a, b, c).

The "old face" is found in the second miniature (Pilate); in the sixth (Nicodemus) and in the seventh (Joseph of Arimathaea and Nicodemus). Here again the three faces are unmistakably related, and the differences come first from the various hats they wear and secondly from the fact that these faces are placed on either straight or rounded backs. And, of course, as was the case for the "young faces", the "old faces" if drawn similarly, display extremely varied expressions. (See illustration II a, b, c, d). It is also interesting to note the similarity of expression in the only two profiles found in these miniatures: the soldier arresting Jesus in the first miniature, and the varlet on the right in the "scourging": the strong jaw-line and thin long lips are quite brutally convincing.

The drawing of the feet is more complex. It would seem that two types of feet were drawn (as we shall see later this would indeed go towards confirming my contention that these seven miniatures are the work of more than one artist). We have what I shall call the "rounded" and the "pointed" feet. The first are seen in the first two miniatures (see illustration III, a, b) and the "pointed" feet are seen in the third and fourth miniatures (illustration

IV, a, b, c). It is also interesting to note that a MS. of the *Histoire du Bon Roi Alexandre* (Paris, Petit Palais, Collection Dutuit, MS. 456), reputed to have been painted in the workshop of Guillaume Vrelant, shows feet painted very similarly to the pointed feet of the Boston MS. It is particularly interesting to compare illustration IVa and illustration V b.

It also happens that figures are drawn in a manner so closely similar as to preclude any coincidence. For instance, one soldier in the first miniature (at the extreme right of the group) and one in the second miniature (at the extreme left of the group) illustrate this point. Although they are drawn "mirror-image", the stance and placing of the arms is the same. The small differences are confined to the armour and the curvature of each sword (see illustration VI, a, b). The "mirror-image" is most probably the proof that the draughtsman used a transparent pattern. James Douglas Farquhar studies this aspect of draughtsmanship at length[7] and indicates several ways of obtaining a tracing medium. According to him the most readily available medium was parchment "scraped very thin". The artist could also make his *carta lustra* in various ways, for instance with glue or with oiled paper.

The grouping of weapons in three of the miniatures (1, 2 and 4) is also extremely interesting: they are displayed in the same order (especially in miniatures 1 and 4) and are similarly angulated. Moreover, in all three cases, they appear grouped "en faisceau" above the heads of each group of soldiers (see illustration VII, a, b, c).

The trees are drawn in two ways in the Boston Manuscript; or, to be more precise, they are either drawn or sketched. The former type can be divided into two categories: as exemplified by the trees in the first miniature and by those in the fourth, sixth and seventh miniatures. In both cases we always see two trees, one partially hiding the other. The technique of drawing is the same: the foliage comes down fairly close to the ground and the branch-structure is visible through the foliage which is indicated by "stitch-marks" on the left and horizontal hatchings on the right. The light comes from the left.[8] The difference is that the trees are round in the first miniature and oblong in the others (see illustration VIII, a, b, c).

The sketched type of tree, which is present in miniatures 5, 6 and 7 is found either single or in groups of two or three. It consists of a vertical line to indicate the trunk and a simple hatching, either horizontal or vertical in a round shape, to indicate the foliage; it is always relegated to the background and is used only to confer a certain balance to the masses (see illustration VII d).

These various observations on drawing techniques seem to prove that although they may not have been drawn by one single artist, the miniatures display ample proof of a concern for unity; of a guiding principle no doubt inspired by a very gifted artist.

Delaissé notes[9] that "the Dutch miniaturists did not always use gouache" and he goes on to show how drawing, "through the technique of crosshatching and shading 'renders' surfaces and even volumes that paint can more easily convey". What happens in the Boston Ms? We have here a combination of the uses of both gouache and drawing. The main outlines are rendered in brush and ink. The ink, thus applied on a grey gouache background, can be made to look (a) very dark indeed when strong shadows are required (see, for instance the left leg of the right hand varlet in the third miniature), or (b) almost transparent, as used for instance to show the naked body of Christ on the cross (miniature 5). In this last case, the shape of the body is painted in ochre gouache and the volumes are rendered by brushstrokes of ink of varying degrees of darkness.

The faces are rendered by a different technique: this technique can be particularly well studied in the first miniature, with the faces of Jesus and Judas. First the basic gouache colour is applied. In this case, the face of Jesus is very light with perhaps a slight tinge of pink in the basic white, whereas the face of Judas is definitely dark, and the basic colour is a light terre-de-sienne. Then the hair colour is applied (this is shown by the slight overlapping of hair colour on face colour in the case of Malchus). Then the eyebrows, eyes (upper lid and pupil) and lips are traced by brush-strokes of darker terre-de-sienne. The eyes are then completed by a dot of white (this order of paint application is evident in the fourth miniature: the dot on Jesus' left eye was applied slightly over the vertical line indicating the pupil; this is also the case in several other instances). Only then were the volumes rendered, and this was done by a combination of ink and body-colour. The ink, being more fluid than body-colour, was especially well designed to render "lines" in faces. This is for instance the case for Pilate's face. The artist has rendered the rings under the eyes, the commissures of the mouth and the sharp bridge of the nose with ink and a very fine brush, and, for the nose at least, a two-hair brush as the tracing shows clearly.

One finds this same technique applied, although with less refinement, in the Boston Public Library Ms. 137. It should be noted here that this manuscript has many features in common with our Boston Passion Ms. Apart form the treatment of faces, the *grisaille* is exactly the same blue grey as in the Passion Ms.; the acanthus leaves are treated in a similar manner; the folds of vestments are treated similarly. The main difference between the two manuscripts is that in the Boston 137, gouache achieves an *impasto* quality, whereas in the Boston 129 the gouache, probably applied with sable brushes, has a smooth, light quality. The Boston 137 had been ascribed by Delaissé to the atelier of Guillaume Vrelant.[10]

In concluding these remarks on the technique of drawing and painting, the question again comes to mind: were the seven miniatures the work of a single artist or rather of several? That one manuscript should be decorated by several hands is not uncommon, as Delaissé has noted regarding Ms. II 7619 of the Brussels Royal Library: "The decoration and illustration of these Hours have been clearly divided among different hands...."[11] If we look at the miniatures of the Boston Ms. with this possibility in mind, we discover that several elements (faces, hands, draperies) can be classified as more or less successful.

To begin with, the first miniature is in a class of its own: the composition is superbly balanced: the hill with chalice and host on the left balances the wooden gate with its dovecote; the grouping of persons is at the same time compact and light and, in the group, the perspective is faultless. St. Peter with his raised sword balances the soldier arresting Jesus; the lighted lantern held high by a soldier balances superbly the extinguished lantern of Malchus lying on the ground. The group composed by Jesus, Judas and Malchus which forms the centre of the picture is also masterly and the continuity is conveyed through the right hand of Jesus whose extended forefinger heals Malchus. Also, the half-extended right leg of Malchus balances the left leg of the soldier arresting Jesus. The faces of the four main characters in this miniature are intensely differentiated as to the feelings and emotions they convey. The hands of all the characters are well-articulated and the gestures they achieve are eminently convincing. Finally, the draperies are deep and soft and those of Peter's robe and mantle are particularly noteworthy. Every aspect of composition or detail in this miniature reveals an accomplished artist.

If we now turn to the other six miniatures we certainly notice a similar care in composition and drawing, but the result is inferior. Yet these are not uniformly inferior. Thus in the second miniature, only Pilate's face stands apart by its force of expression; and, leaving aside any judgement of quality, it is evident that Jesus in miniatures 2, 3 and 4 was painted by one artist, and in miniatures 5, 6 and 7 by another: the brush strokes are different; the expression is different. In the "Scourging" the face of the left hand varlet, at the same time angelic and ruthless, has a *modelé* very much akin to the work done in the first miniature.

As to Mary, mother of Jesus, who appears in the last three miniatures, it would seem that one artist was responsible for the work in all of them, but that one artist drew the coif and cloak in miniature 5, and another in the last two.

St. John gets a rough treatment in all three miniatures where he appears. Although in miniature 5 the face is obviously on the model of the first miniature (see illustration I b, and c) in miniatures 6 and 7, his head is at an awkward angle; neither has any volume and very little expression, with the exception perhaps of the last one: here John's expression is one of compassion but it is conveyed through crude lines and, again, the face has no volume.

Much more could be said about the faces, but the hands are even more interesting to study. It is impossible to establish a pattern. As in the faces, there are some good and some bad elements side by side in the same miniature. Generally speaking the hands are very poorly drawn and also too small in comparison with the bodies. In the second and third miniatures they are all poor, except for the hands (and arms) of the left varlet (min. 3) which are a direct transfer of Peter's in the first miniature. In fact, the similarity extends to the whole figure in both cases (see illustration IX a, b). The hands in the "carrying of the Cross" are extremely interesting in that some are very well sketched, but the work stops there: no *modelé*, no volumes. It would seem that the artist of the first miniature sketched the hands of the leading soldier at least (as well as the whole figure) but that the artist who was given the task of finishing the work was not up to it and sensibly left things in the sketchy stage rather than risk spoiling the whole work. In the fifth miniature the hands of Christ curling around the nails are well-drawn but all others are hopelessly inadequate: they are generally too small and completely unconvincing.

It would seem that the draperies in the last six miniatures suffer from the same trouble that besets the hands in the fourth one: the technique of folds in the cloth is the same but whereas the impression given in the first miniature is superbly convincing, that in the others remains flat and stiff.

We can conclude from these observations that the set of miniatures of the Boston Manuscript was not the work of a single artist. That the master produced the first one and either sketched or gave indications for the others, indications which were inconsistently applied due to the partial lack of artistic talent in the collaborators.

3.   *Compositional Style*

The seven miniatures of the Boston *Passion* are not a social document. The artist and his collaborators were only concerned in depicting the suffering of Jesus. "Jesus n'enseigne plus, il souffre" notes Emile Mâle[12] and, he adds: "on dirait que la chrétienté tout entière reçoit le don des larmes". The pictures are meant to move us, to make us weep. Jesus is always at the centre of the picture and all other characters are grouped around him, either to inflict the suffering or to reveal it. Indeed, if one draws diagonal lines across each miniature, one becomes aware that Jesus' head in the first six miniatures is in the upper triangle;

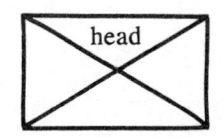

in the last miniature, Mary occupies the position of Jesus. And in five out of seven miniatures, the lines join at the level of the solar plexus. This device which focuses the attention on Jesus and the elements which reinforce this trend are almost too numerous to instance.

I spoke at length earlier of the wonderful sense of balance to be found in the first miniature: a balance with a sense of purpose.

The same is true of the other miniatures. In the scene before Pilate, Jesus is at the very centre of a group of soldiers and this is reïnforced by the weapons whose "faisceau" joins fictitiously at Jesus' shoulder. The round-shaped group is counterbalanced by the elongated and lonely figure of Pilate.

In the "scourging", the centrality of Jesus is achieved in the antithesis of movement (of the varlet) and immobility (of Jesus). This movement is achieved by an extremely simple device: each varlet holds an end of the rope which binds Christ to the column, and this rope is convex between one varlet and Jesus and concave between the other varlet and Jesus. Moreover, the whips they each brandish are so angulated as to point fictitiously at Jesus' head.

In the "Carrying of the Cross" this effect is achieved by two soldiers: one leading, dragging Jesus, the other pushing, prodding him. It is further enhanced by the contrast between the cross which conveys an impression of dead weight and Jesus himself who is drawn in an almost transparent manner.

The apparent simplicity of the miniature representing the "Death on the Cross" is deceptive, for whatever way one chooses to connect the directional lines on the picture (and there are numerous ways of doing this), one is always brought back to Jesus. Everything is static here. The spaces between the figures are very great and the whole scene conveys a sense of the immensity of the void created by the death of Christ. "Un film dont le son s'est enrayé" says Anouilh in the Prologue of *Antigone*. Indeed suspension of sound and movement now that the Word, the Life has died.

In the following miniature, the sinuous, feminine movement of the "Descent from the Cross" leads to Mary whose Passion now holds the centre of the stage. Even though the drawing of individual features is faulty (Jesus is too small; the hands are generally unconvincing etc.), this does not detract from the essential message.

In the last miniature, the figures are now grouped around Mary, yet she is not at the centre of a circle but at one end of an ovoid, bending, straining towards Jesus. Vertically, the cross balances the unction stone and, horizontally, Joseph and Nicodemus balance each other. And the result is a double focus: a dynamic one with Mary and a static one with Jesus.

This very brief survey of a few of the aspects which constitute the strength of the compostional technique of these miniatures will nonetheless suffice to show the remarkable sense of purpose which presided in the mind of the artist and his collaborators. Claude Bragdon, in his masterly study *The Beautiful Necessity*, sums up this sense of purpose in these words:

> A work of art is nothing if not artful: like an acrostic, the more different ways it can be read - up, down, across, from right to left and from left to right - the better it is, other things being equal. This statement, of course, may be construed in such a way as to appear absurd; what is meant is simply that the more a work of art is freighted and fraught with meaning beyond meaning, the more secure its immortality, the more powerful its appeal. For enjoyment, it is not necessary that all these meanings should be fathomed, it is only necessary that they should be felt.[13]

The seven miniatures find an echo both in their general composition and in their details, in Ms. 439 of the Walters Art Gallery (W.A.G.), Baltimore. Fol. 28r of this Ms. (reproduced here, Plate IX) gives a miniature of the crucifixion (introducing the *Stabat Mater*) surrounded by six medallions representing various episodes of the Passion. They should be looked at anti-clockwise, from the bottom of the page up. The first one represents Jesus praying in the Garden of Olives which our manuscript does not have and the "Descent from the Cross" is not represented. Otherwise the other five medallions correspond to the miniatures of the *Passion* Ms. But the correspondence goes well beyond one confined merely to subject matter; indeed the composition is absolutely similar in both manuscripts. It is interesting to note that the carrying of the cross presents a "mirror-image" of our manuscript. If only one of the medallions had corresponded in its composition to a *Passion* miniature, one might have thought of a coincidence, but since all miniatures correspond, coincidence has to be ruled out. It is indeed highly probable that both workshops used the same set of patterns and, in view of the "mirror-image" of the "Carrying of the Cross" the set was probably on *carta lustra*. The composition in these medallions goes so far as to present the same feature as the Boston Ms. 129: namely the head of Christ is always situated in the upper triangle of any diagonal division, with the exception (as in the Boston Ms. 129) of the "entombment". It would be vain to speculate as to which of the two manuscripts is the older, and, indeed, it would prove nothing. Suffice it to say that the W.A.G. Ms. 439 had been made for the Earl of Lamarck and Cleves who married the daughter of Jehan-Sans-Peur. His motto was: *Plus quonques mes*. It is a prayer-book in honour of the Virgin and contains (fol.100) the Hours of the Virgin. The Rubrics are in French. The use is that of the archdiocese of Cambrai with a few antiphons for the use of Arras and Amiens. Each folio measures 120 x 170 mm. and each medallion measures 23 to 30 x 29 to 40 mm.

To conclude these observations, let us consider in what spirit these miniatures were painted. The most searching analysis has been made by Delaissé in his book: *A Century of Dutch Manuscript Illumination*. Speaking of Dutch art in the middle of the XVth century, he observes:

> The subjects are conceived and rendered with simplicity and naturalness: landscapes with a low horizon, people with individuality, gestures and attitudes correctly observed - in a word all the usual qualities of the northern miniatures.

And he adds:

> They are not sterotyped puppets, neither idealized nor made vulgar, neither lifeless nor exuberant; they are simple human beings.[14]

He also notes the "sincerity and sensitivity in the portrayal of human actions"[15] and the "homogeneity" and "spontaneity"[16] found in the work of Dutch miniaturists.

All these qualifications fit our set of paintings excellently: they never represent a social document. Indeed, the spiritual and psychological realism which I noted in connexion with the commentary on the text applies here and the remarks made there concerning their obvious link with the *Devotio Moderna* are equally true as regards the art of the miniatures. Delaissé felt that the *Devotio Moderna* could be "considered one of the most vital changes in the spiritual life of Western Europe." and that it was "as devoid of allegory as Dutch manuscript illumination is of abtruse symbolism". No observations could fit this set of paintings more aptly.

4.   *Decoration*

A study of the decoration of the manuscript (frames, floral border and initials) will, through comparison with other manuscripts, help to complement the various observations made above.

Each miniature is inscribed in a very plain frame of mauve delimited by black lines. The two bands of mauve are separated by a very thin gold line. In the case of the first miniature, the setting is more elaborate: the miniature is also set into a large frame, open at the top and comprising the first verse of the poem with its decorated initial. This, in its turn is surrounded by an unframed floral border. This second larger frame is interrupted on the left by the decorated initial, and its vertical sides stop slightly above the top of the framed miniature (about 1 mm). The devices which consist in leaving the outer frame open and in interrupting it for the decorated initial confer on the whole composition a sense of lightness which is extremely pleasing. The outer frame has the same structure as the frames for the miniatures. This very particularized setting is strongly reminiscent of no less famous a manuscript than the *Bréviaire de Phillippe le Bon* (Brussels, Royal library Ms. 9511). Not only are the setting and design similar but the colours are also the same. The same settings and designs are also found in the *Heures dites de Charles le Téméraire* (Copenhagen, Royal Library Ms. 1612). Leroquais[17] has identified these manuscripts as coming from the hands or the workshop of Guillaume Vrelant.

The floral border here is painted directly onto the parchment and not on a monochrome or washed gold background as became the current practice after 1475.[18] The acanthus leaves, penned *rinceaux* and tendrils are extremely light and, in that, differ from the treatment they are given in many manuscripts of the same period and provenance where they are often overwhelmingly heavy and tend to distract from the miniature they frame. Here, on the contrary, the border constitutes an uplift to the miniature. The *rinceaux* and tendrils are sparingly interspersed with stylised flowers. They are in dark magenta, mauve and blue and the pistils are occasionally painted white. The acanthus leaves are blue, dotted with white, and their curlicues end in washed gold or sand colour. The leaves, of which there are very few, are dull green. The gold dots along the tendrils are burnished and lightly circled in penned black ink. The overall effect of the floral border is one of exquisite lightness. It virtually creates the impression that the border hovers above the page and it is a fitting accompaniment to the miniature with its overall effect of subtle *chiaroscuro*. Prof. Robert Calkins, (Cornell University), a specialist on XVth cent. manuscript illumination, in a personal communication, said he was of the opinion that the border was more Flemish than Dutch and was typical of the early Bruges period (1445 - 48). The acanthus leaves are treated similarly in the Boston Ms. 137 and, in some places, in the Holkham Hall Ms. 48 (a Book of Hours) although here the leaves are painted deep black and gold and are so large in relation to the miniature that they overwhelm it. Both Mss. are attributed by Delaissé to the workshop of Guillaume Vrelant. Similar borders can also be found in Munich (Bayerische Staatsbibl. Cod. gall. 40) and in Brussels (Royal Library Ms. 11105 - 11105 fol 66). These last two manuscripts are attributed to Guillaume Vrelant. A similar border can also be found in a Flemish Ms., W.A.G. Ms. 190 and in W.A.G. Ms. 197, dated about 1456/9, another Flemish manuscript from the workshop of Guillaume Vrelant. It is interesting to note that Vrelant's imitators paint borders which are far heavier and uninspired (see, for instance the cod. gall. 28 of the Munich Staatsbibl.: *Traités ascétiques*).

The decorated initials are used for the first letter after a miniature only. In the first one, it encroaches upon the second border and interrupts it. They alternate blue on a mauve background and mauve on a blue background. The shape of the letter is traced in white and gold and the thick parts are filled with geometrical designs: waves with dots and affronted angles. The centres are filled with convoluted painted *rinceaus* ending in trefoil leaves (symbol of the Trinity) and the tip of each lobe is touched with white or gold. Initials exactly similar to this are found abundantly in the Brussels Royal Library Ms. 9511, and also in the Holkham Hall Ms. 48 and in the Boston Ms. 137. We also find an identical initial in W.A.G. Ms. 190 fol. 36r. Two more examples should be noted. First a Victoria and Albert Museum Ms.: A.L. 1686-1902 (Reid Ms. 48) of Flemish origin with initials very similar to our Ms. and a manuscript in the Sotheby sales of 1st December, 1956 *ex* Dyson Perrins, Lot 78. It is a book of Hours of the Virgin for the use of Rome, illuminated by Guillaume Vrelant. Here the capitals are absolutely identical.

5. *Settings*

Under this heading are included such elements as can identify or date the manuscript but do not form an essential part of the decoration. They include a study of trees, towns and landscapes; 'props' (such as palisade; dovecote; chalice and wafer; column; scallop on hat and Mary's coif) and mainly *militaria* and costumes.

The trees in our manuscript have been described at length earlier in this chapter. It was noted then that the foliage is treated as a mass. Studying the same aspect in other manuscripts, Byvanck notes[19]: "les enlumineurs des Pays-Bas septentrionaux traitent généralement l'ensemble du feuillage comme une masse rehaussée de quelques reflets de lumière". This could not describe our trees more aptly. Trees similarly treated are found in profusion in the Brussels Bibliothèque Royale Ms. 10173-4 and 9263 (painted in Bruges) and in Ms. 9511 (which has already been mentioned on various occasions) and again in the W.A.G. Ms. 197 also mentioned earlier. It would seem that this kind of tree was typical of the Vrelant atelier, although other types were also used besides.[20]

In all outdoor miniatures we have landscapes with a low horizon. No effort is made to identify or individualize them. The hills and towns are credible but unidentifiable and are truly there as a 'prop' and no more. A low horizon is of course typical of Dutch landscapes and the absence of detail has been noted by Byvanck: "Le désir d'introduire le paysage ne se manifeste nulle part"[21]. In fact, even in the first miniature where so much more care and artistry is present than in the other six miniatures, the landscape is reduced to two hills whose volumes are indicated by cross-hatchings executed in a summary fashion. Thus we can say that as they stand almost by default, the elements of landscape point to a Dutch origin.

The 'props' yield better circumstantial evidence: The circular wooden palisade with portal and dovecote cannot be said to be typical of one region more than another and it can be seen on numerous manuscripts: French, Flemish and Dutch. E. Mâle[22] notes their presence in Bourdichon, and Hubert Caillaux in his illustration of the *Mystère de Valenciennes* and elsewhere. It was a traditional setting. The only observation to be made here is that it is more usual to see a wattle fence in French (Paris and Touraine) manuscripts, and a wooden palisade with portal in Northern ones. Identical palisades can be seen in The British Library Ms. Royal 15 D. 1, of Flemish origin, and in the Ushaw College Ms. 10, a Book of Hours *ad usum Angliae* also of Flemish origin. In the Boston Public Library Ms. 172 we again see the same type of spiked wooden fence with portal. Here all the miniatures are in colour. The manuscript was manufactured at the Cloister of Agnietenberg, near Zwolle *ca.* 1480.

The chalice and wafer start to appear only in the XIVth century. Louis Réau notes[23]: "A partir du XIVe siècle ils (=the artists) représentent presque toujours, dans les scènes de l'Agonie [...] un calice posé sur un rocher avec une hostie suspendue au-dessus." This setting is present in the W.A.G. Ms. 439 discussed earlier, and in numerous other manuscripts. In the Holkham Hall Ms. 48 fol. 8 representing St. John on Patmos, the chalice has exactly the same shape and stands in the same manner as ours.

The column of the scourging is very slender in our manuscript. It has no architectural function whereas in the *Milan Hours* of the Turin Museo Civico Ms., the column painted in the historiated N is an integral part of the architecture of the room. Yet, in both cases the artistic concept is the same: 2 varlets turning around Jesus and brandishing their whips; similar paving etc. I feel that the artistic concept in the Boston Manuscript is more consistent with the general trend of the whole set of paintings in that no extraneous element is allowed to distract the eye from the essentials whereas in the Turin Ms., the rather elaborate architecture does distract the attention from the essentials. The Turin-Milan Hours Ms., completed about 1445, is the work of Dutch artists.[24] Regarding this Réau notes[25] that Levitic Law prescribed the scourging of the patient lying down and the Roman Law, standing. He also notes that the tall thin column is a product of the late middle ages and that it was inspired by the column shown to pilgrims to Jerusalem in the Franciscan chapel of the Holy Sepulchre.

The scallop shell sewn onto the hat of one of the assistants was of course part of the traditional dress of the mediaeval pilgrim to Compostella. It appears in various manuscripts and can be found in the Boston Ms. 137 and in the Holkham Ms. 48.

Mary's vestment in the last three miniatures consists of a large veil which envelops her completely and the artist could well have been inspired by Pseudo-Anselm's description of it: "Quadam veste [...] qua tegitur caput et totum corpus, et est quasi linteum". Yet, this "shroud" is not simply put on the head, but stands on a stiff coif of a kind that recalls the headdress worn by the Béguines since their foundation in 1245 right up to the present day. A similar coif is represented in both Holkham Ms. 48 and Boston Ms. 137.

Regarding *militaria* and costumes, E. Mâle notes[26]: "Au XVe siècle, dans les scènes de la Passion, les soldats romains portent l'armure de la fin du moyen âge. L'art suit les progrès du costume militaire".

For the sake of clarity, I have divided this phase of the study into the following categories: weapons; head-gears; armour; civilian costume.

Each type of weapon is found in the first miniature and repeated with one exception in "Jesus before Pilate" and "Jesus carrying his cross".

The Weapons

In *"Jesus in the garden of Gethsemane"*
St. Peter's sword: a stiff-bladed sword with wheel-pommel; late 14th century (see Wilkinson XIX, 1)[27] although in the miniature the quillon appears to be straight instead of very slightly down-curving: a straight quillon might indicate an *estoc* but then Peter's sword is not long enough for an *estoc*. Moreover Peter's pommel has definitely no button and on Wilkinson's XIX, 2 the pommel has a button. Peter's sword is also similar to Wilkinson's XXI: a cut-and-thrust sword, late 14th or early 15th century, but here there is a faint suggestion of a button on the pommel and the quillon's ends are hooked.

Soldier's sword: in fact, a falchion "one of the earliest of curved swords in Europe" (Wilkinson at XXXIX). A rather beautiful and elaborate example occurs in Wilkinson's XXXII, although of a later date (mid-16th century).
Soldier's weapons (left to right) (these are staff- or pole-arms):

(a) *mace* "no more than a stout stick reinforced at one end by a head bristling with spikes" (Martin p. 243)[28]

(b) *bill* (see Wilkinson XXXVI, b and d) and (Martin 221) although on our miniature the blade is more separate from the haft (see fig. 19 p. 246 in Martin: Burgundian Archers and Spearmen by Master W. A. *ca*. 1475): one very similar;

(c) *pitchfork* or *fourche ferrée* (see Martin 215);

(d) *voulge* see Martin p. 238: "This weapon was adopted in 1468 for the "Body Archers" of the great Bastard Anthony of Burgundy as well as in the Burgundian army in general when they used it against the Swiss at the battles of Grandson, Morat and Nancy in 1476-1477";

(e) unidentifiable as it is only partially seen, but probably a *battle axe on pole* (see Martin 115);

(f) "*morning star*" *mace* (see Wilkinson 28a).

Martin (p. 237) speaks of "the difficulty of identifying exactly any type of staff-weapon and to classify it in its appropriate category, since many are hybrids and do not fall into any definite class."

In "*Jesus carrying his cross*"
(from left to right) the weapons are mace, fourche ferrée, mace and voulge; two others are unidentifiable; morning star, battle-axe: "it was still in existence and used in the wars of the 15th century" (Martin p. 248).

In "*Jesus before Pilate*"
The weapons are: mace; voulge and, perhaps a bill-XVth century-(see Martin 221); also, one soldier has a falchion.

The head-gears

In "*Jesus in the Garden of Gethsemane*":
closed headgear: the great bascinet is Burgundian (see Martin 150: from 1500; and 151: early XVth century);

all the others: "about the middle of the 15th century [...] another form of head protection made its appearance. The sallet generally took the shape of an almost spherical headdress [...] it partly covered the back of the neck [...] it was adopted towards the second third of the 15th century [...] in France" (Martin pp. 136-137; see also Martin 153 and 154).

Michèle Beaulieu[29] has found head-gears with both closed and open visors in two 1468 Mss. The first is from Breslau T.2. fol. 287; it is a copy of Froissart's *Chronicles* and the second is from the Arsenal, Paris Ms. 5073 fol. 2, in the second volume of Renaud de Montauban. She also notes a *salade à rouelle* in the Dutuit Ms. 456 fol. 68. (*Livre des conquètes d'Alexandre*, 1448: a manuscript to which we have had occasion to refer several times). There is a particularly good example of such a *salade* in our fourth miniature (soldier on the extreme left).

The armour

According to Bruhn and Tilke (38.2)[30] the foot-soldiers wear armour of *circa* 1430 - and some pieces could even go back as far as the end of the XIVth century. This applies to the breastplates, couters, pauldrons, gauntlets, sabatons, lance-rests, vambraces and armbraces, but "sheer necessity, coupled with the insecurity of the times and the prices charged for a complete set of accoutrements, often caused a suit of armour to be worn as long as it remained serviceable, even after it had become out of date". (Martin p. 70). One should also note the soft skirts worn by the foot-soldiers which are similar to that worn by one of the Knights of Christ in St. Bavon's church panel by Jan van Eyck 1430 - 1440.[31] There are excellent examples of pauldrons, couters and side-wides similar to those worn in the first and fourth miniatures noted by M. Beaulieu. They can be found respectively in the Brussels Ms. Royal Library 6 fol. 151v. (this *Histoire de Charles Martel* was painted in Bruges by Loiset Lyedet and dates from 1463-70); in the Bibliothèque Nationale Paris Ms. fr. 9199 which was painted in Bruges in 1469 (this superb manuscript in *grisaille* was executed for Louis de Bruges by Jean Miélot); in Brussels, Royal Library Ms. 5392 fol. 6v. (it is the *Epitre d'Othea* and dates from 1461). Martin says that there is no complete armour of that time in any public or private collection; only pieces and fragments (see Martin p. 76). Also:

> "it should not be forgotten that the ordinary men-at-arms, whether mounted or dismounted, wore somewhat dissimilar types adapted to their particular function as pikemen, halberdiers, crossbowmen, archers and others". (Martin p. 77).

In the XIVth century, articulated gauntlets were made of whalebone, iron or brass.[32] Here they are not spiked (this is a XVth century invention). Elsewhere he says: "The foot-soldiers of the period had long adopted a form of demi-cuirass, covering the body and thighs, but leaving entire freedom of movements to the legs and arms." (Martin p. 87.)

The civilian costumes

These are almost non-existent in our set of miniatures; yet the few items that appear in the various pictures are consistent in style and in date.

The shoes worn by servants in the "Scourging" are the type called "à la poulaine". A. Harmand states several times[33] that they were worn around 1450 and E. Mâle indicates precisely that they were no longer worn after 1480 [34], and according to Bruhn and Tilke (47.4), they were worn around 1460.

All the other items of civilian costume: peaked caps made of beaver or felt (Pilate), with narrow or wide brims (Joseph of Arimathea, Nicodemus, one retainer)[35]; the long coat slit from the waist down, (mahoître); and the elbow cape, can be seen again in the *Histoire de Charles Martel* painted at Bruges by Loiset Lyedet between 1463 and 1470. The scenes represent a reception at the court of Burgundy. The mahoître can also be seen in the Bibliothèque Nationale Ms. fr. 9198. It contains the *Miracles of Notre Dame*. It was commissioned by Louis de Bruges and executed in 1456. Thus all the items of civilian costume point to a date of execution somewhere between 1450 and 1470. If we add to this the evidence furnished by weapons and armour we can infer that the manuscript was painted between 1461 and 1469 and that it shows Burgundian influence.

6. *Hagiological elements*

In the masterly study: "*Circumdederunt me canes multi*"[36] James Marrow shows the importance of extra-evangelical accretions to the narrative of the Passion in the late middle ages, and studies the importance of Psalm 21 on the one hand, and of Netherlandish Passion literature on the other. He speaks of "the desire of pious men and women to approach the divine through intimate knowledge and empathic experience of Christ's humanity and Passion."[37] These remarks are indeed in full accordance with our own findings. Yet it is important to note once again, that neither in the text studied here, nor in the miniatures of the Boston manuscript is the emphasis placed on the physical tormentors of Christ. Both chose rather to rouse compassion by displaying the emotional suffering of Christ.

To achieve this without the obvious help of gross torture, called for a strong reliance on symbolic features. Some elements are accretions almost contemporary to the painting of the pictures; others have their roots in much earlier times. A few of these elements will be discussed here.

Judas is often represented less tall than Jesus. Réau[38] refers the origin of this practice to St. Birget's *Revelations*. Here, it is not the case: Judas is practically as tall as Jesus, but the element of meanness is present nonetheless. It is conveyed by a certain roundness of the shoulders, a sideways look, a sallow complexion and generally speaking, an air of cowardly subservience fully in contrast with Jesus' erect figure and youthful attitude.

In the same miniature, we have two lanterns and these are found traditionally in this scene although quite often, the lantern carried here by a soldier is replaced by a torch, in accordance with the johannic tradition. (See for instance Walters Art Gallery Baltimore, Ms. 168 and Landes-Museum Münster, Book of Hours of Catherine of Lockhorst. etc....). Studying the influence of theatre production on the visual arts, E. Mâle[39] notes that the lantern is absent from the arts in the first part of the XIVth century; it appears at the beginning of the XVth century and continues until the middle of the XVIth century; here the soldier carries a lighted lantern, whereas Malchus' lantern is upset on the ground and extinguished. Yet these lanterns are more than a 'prop' and their spiritual symbolism is evident.

The fourth miniature, "Jesus carrying his Cross" is perhaps the one most akin to coeval iconography: Jesus really appears to be faltering under the weight of the cross and He is leashed to a bragging soldier who symbolically brandishes the three nails of the crucifixion. There is also a third element which enhances Jesus' suffering and humiliation and is very much in line with the then current custom of emphasizing this aspect of the Passion: a soldier, behind Jesus, viciously pulls his hair and hits him behind with his knee. I have found the same gesture in a manuscript in the Walters Art Gallery, Baltimore, Ms. 185, fol. 65v. This is a Dutch manuscript painted around 1415-20 for the family of Orlencourt near St. Omer. The Hours are for the use of the Diocese of Utrecht. In this, as in the Boston Ms., all the elements bear a human interest and, as Dorothy Miner puts it, "the scenes are presented with the minimum of accoutrement".[40]

The representation of Nicodemus and Joseph of Arimathaea in the scenes of the Descent from the Cross and the Entombment is quite complex. E. Mâle,[41] developing his contention that the theatre influenced painters in the way they represented Joseph and Nicodemus, observes that Nicodemus is always old and bearded while Joseph is always young and shaven. He adds that this applies to Flemish and German works of art but not often to French art where both men are old and bearded. An exception to this is the Holy Sepulchre group at Solesmes. Here Nicodemus has a beard and Joseph is shaven. This classification is denied by both L. Réau and G. Millet. Studying the Descent from the Cross in a Greek manuscript - which he later calls "byzantin" - from Florence, illustrated in the Xth century (no other indication given) Réau writes[42]:

> "Joseph d'Arimathie soutient le corps du Christ pendant que Nicodème arrache le clou de la main gauche. Le bras droit est déjà détaché; it pendrait inerte si la Vierge, par un mouvement où la tendresse s'unit au respect, ne le saisissait de ses mains voilées et ne l'approchait de sa bouche".

and, further on, he notes that in Occidental art the hands of the Virgin are never veiled.

This presentation: Joseph holding the body of Jesus; Nicodemus on a ladder removing the left-hand nail and Mary seizing the hand of Jesus, is upheld by G. Millet[43] who calls this style byzantine - and it agrees completely with our seventh miniature. But then, who is the kneeling figure removing the nail from the feet? It appears that, for a time, Nicodemus held this position. The three men in our miniature seem to be of equal social rank and, although the possibility of this figure or the one on the ladder, representing a retainer, should not be discounted outright, is it not possible that the artist unwittingly represented Nicodemus twice, once at the left hand and once at the feet? This would show the combination of the form where no one is yet represented at the feet and the form where no one is any longer at the left hand.

Turning now to the scene of the Entombment, L. Réau[44] notes that, according to established protocol, Joseph is at the head and Nicodemus at the feet of Christ. This would contradict E. Mâle's idea of a young Joseph and an old Nicodemus. In any case, in our miniature, both men are bearded and both look old. If we go by their head-dress and compare it with those in the preceding miniature, we see that the upturned brim was worn by Joseph and therefore that Joseph is, on our last miniature, at the head of Jesus, while Nicodemus, with the peaked cap, is at the feet. It also shows that, in the preceding miniature, Nicodemus who, there also, wears the peaked cap, removes the nail from the feet, which leaves the rôle of the man on the ladder either to another Nicodemus (following the hypothesis proposed above) or simply to a retainer. In favour of this last hypothesis it may be pointed out that the man on the ladder is beardless whereas the two bearded men of the seventh miniature are portrayed similarly in the eighth miniature.

In the last miniature, Jesus is represented naked, save for a loincloth, lying on the shroud which is placed on what is commonly called the unction stone. This unction stone has known a curious fortune and E. Mâle describes its evolution in art at length.[45] Briefly, byzantine art represented Jesus on the unction stone stained with Mary's tears. This stone was venerated in the Pantocrator Church in Constantinople. But the Italians, who did not know about the unction stone, saw in it a sarcophagus, and represented the Entombment. In the majority of XVth century representations of the Entombment, Christ is being lowered into the open Sepulchre by Joseph and Nicodemus who hold him on the shroud, while Mary and John and, occasionally, the Holy Women watch and lament. This is for instance the case of the Paris Arsenal Ms. 575 fol. 132: of the New York Pierpont Morgan Ms. 87 fol. 200v.; of the Brussels, Royal Library Ms. 21696 fol. 50v. and IV 194 fol. 59; of the Oxford, Bodleian Library Ms. Auct. D. inf. 2. 13 fol. 102v.etc.). In the Boston Ms, on the contrary, Jesus is being laid on top of a flat surface which could be either a representation of the unction stone, in which case Joseph and Nicodemus are redundant, or onto what could be the lid of the sarcophagus, but, in this case the gesture of the two men is inexplicable, for why should Jesus be laid on top of the sarcophagus when they would later have to deposit the body elsewhere in order to open the sarcophagus? We may well be confronted here with a corruption of the two forms.

On the other side of the sepulchre are six figures. First, Mary who, in a gesture full of tenderness holds the right hand of her son against her cheek and, beside her, John who tries to comfort her and, perhaps hold her back. These two figures are commonly found in this context. Behind them come four more figures (and not three), all women wearing the high coif and long veil of the *Béguines*. This is unusual. E. Mâle[46] also notes four women in the group of the deposition at Eu. He identifies them as Mary Salome; Mary Jacobi; Martha and Magdalen. Jean Michel in his *Passion* also places four women with Mary and John. One of them, in the mind of the Boston manuscript painter, may possibly have been meant to represent the person who commissioned the miniatures, but this is only conjecture.

7. *The evidence from the tunic of Malchus*

In the first miniature, Malchus is depicted fallen to the ground and facing us. His tunic bears the initials AF on its front with a knot between them (see illustration X a). This is certainly the most tempting morsel of evidence for very few artists signed their work in those days, and Prof. Calkins talks of "the prevailing anonymity of the medieval artist."[47] The few miniatures which bear a signature do so either plainly, at the end of the book ("I, so and so, finished this work at...on...etc..) or, by some device in one of the miniatures of the manuscript: it can be found either in the border of vestments, or on pavings, or on the flaps of royal tents, etc. Here the AF drawn on the front of the servant's tunic is very much in evidence. Another

AF group, absolutely identical (see illustration X b) can be found on the paving of a miniature in the *Histoire du Bon Roi Alexandre*, Ms. 456 of the Dutuit collection, a manuscript we have already studied at length during the course of this study. In this manuscript the mark is found on fol. 12. F. de Mély made an extensive study of that manuscript's inscriptions.[48] Trying to identify the AF in question, he searched the Bruges list of artists and made various suggestions, but without much success, since the only possible artist would be Anthonin Fieret, but he worked in Tournai in 1488. He also mentions the *obit* of Fraet Alexandre. In 1910, V. Leroquais took up the challenge of this inscription in his *Bréviaire de Philippe le Bon*.[49] He reads on the pavings the initials AE (not AF) which he equates with *Alexandre*. I have carefully looked at the miniature and can in no way see an E in any of the paving stones where the cypher appears. Indeed the F is in all cases absolutely identical to the one found in the Boston manuscript. Is it possible to identify the cypher? Several anonymous articles which appeared in *Le Beffroi* for 1872/3 may help to throw some light on this problem. In "Documents inédits sur les enlumineurs de Bruges" (pp. 111 *ff.*) we find the name of Antoine de Fontaines in the accounts of the guild of St. John the Evangelist founded by Guillaume Vrelant in Bruges in 1454. Fontaines appears in 1478-9 when he is received in the guild and pays a fee of 12 guilders; in 1480 he pays his dues: 6 guilders; again in 1480, he introduces a new member: Colin de la Hoye, who pays 6 guilders; and in 1485 he is recorded again as having paid 6 guilders for his dues. In view of the preceding study which led us to believe that the manuscript was probably manufactured in the 1460s, this name comes rather late. Yet we have many times noted the affinity of our Ms. with the work of the Vrelant workshop, in whose guild Fontaines worked. If Fontaines joined the guild already as a full-fledged artist then the Boston Ms. may be one of his first works - it is just possible, but would he have been in charge of a section of the workshop, as our study suggests that the artist who painted (and signed) the first miniature was? Again, this is possible if he joined the guild as an already accomplished artist. Unfortunately no evidence can be advanced to confirm this and it seems impossible to carry this line of argument further.

Another possibility suggests itself from the perusal of an article in the same *Beffroi*. It is an anonymous study entitled "Le Palais du Franc à Bruges".[50] On p. 76, we read: "En 1445, on fit couvrir le buffet, les sièges et les bancs de la salle de conseil avec du drap rouge de Tournai orné d'un semis de six cents fleurs brodées et de vingt-neuf médaillons avec de grands écussons armoyés: ces broderies furent exécutées par Pierre van Mesne d'après les dessins du peintre Alexandre Fraet"; this name is certainly the same as the Fraet Alexandre whose dateless obituary Mely discovered. The accounts of the Franc for the period 11 Sept. 1445 to 9 Sept. 1445 [51] do not mention Alexandre's salary or, in fact, any other detail. Could he, perhaps, have been the artist who painted the first of the Boston Ms. miniatures, and who directed a workshop of his own? It is not impossible. In order to have been entrusted with the design for the Franc Palace in Bruges, his reputation must already have been well-established and the dates are, of course, consistent with the ones suggested for our manuscript. But here again, we can go no further.

In conclusion we may quote V. Leroquais, who had such an extensive knowledge of manuscripts and was more than anyone aware of the problems besetting this kind of research: "L'intérêt (est de) [...] grouper un ensemble de manuscrits dont la décoration présente des affinités réelles, [...] de mettre en lumière des analogies de composition et des comparaisons et, en définitive, de faire mieux connaître l'oeuvre d'un maître, d'un atelier ou d'une école."[52] This is what we have endeavoured to do all along this study.

Thus we have learnt that the miniatures displayed a strong Netherlandish influence tempered with Flemish characteristics; that, it could be compared from compositional, stylistic and technical standpoints with works produced by the workshop of Guillaume Vrelant; the evidence adduced from the floral border shows that it must have been manufactured between 1448-50 and 1475, and, as adduced from the study of *militaria* and costumes, most likely between 1461 and 1469. If the evidence given by the identity of the scribe (see chapter: Description and history of the manuscripts) is also added, it is possible further to pinpoint the date as being between 1467 and 1469. Finally, one name emerges as that of a possible artist: Alexandre Fraet.

NOTES

1. Munich Staatsbibliothek MS. Germ. 1102.

2. The question as to whether Jesus was crucified with three or four nails was hotly debated in the Middle Ages. See particularly Cornelius Curtius, *De clavis Dominicis Liber...* Antwerp, 1670. See also our chapter 4.

3. M. Teasdale Smith, "The use of grisaille as a lenten observance" in *Marsyas* vol: VIII, 1957, p. 51.

4. L.M.J. Delaissé, *A Century of Dutch Manuscript Illumination.* Berkeley (UCLA Press), 1968, p. 31.

5. See E. Panofski, *Early Netherlandish Painting.* Cambridge, Mass, 1960. p. 161-162; see also C. de Tolnay, *Le Maître de Flémalle.* Bruxelles, 1939, p. 26.

6. The artist was faced with exactly the same problem in the "Descent from the Cross"; this time it is the length of the right arm which was causing him concern and we can also discern five different attempts at solving the length of the horizontal beam.

7. See J.D. Farquhar, *Creation and Imitation.* Nova/NYIT University Press 1976. see: Methods of transferring designs pp. 61 - 69.

8. In all seven miniatures the light comes from the left: the shadow of pebbles, for instance in miniatures 4, 5 and 6 invariably proves this.

9. L.M.J. Delaissé, *op.cit.*, pp. 26 and 27.

10. See note on this manuscript by Z. Haraszty in B. P. L. Quarterly, 1957, p. 62.

11. L.M.J. Delaissé, *op. cit.*, p. 46.

12. E. Mâle, *L'art religieux de la fin du moyen âge en France.* Paris, (A. Colin), 1925, pp. 86 and 87.

13. C. Bragdon, *The Beautiful Necessity.* London n. d. (1st edition 1910), p. 60/61. Bragdon postulates nine "laws" in this report: unity, polarity, trinity, multiplicity in unity, consonance, diversity in monotony, balance, rhythmic change (or diminution) and radiation.

14. L.J.M. Delaissé, *op. cit.*, pp. 41 and 58.

15. *Ibid.*, p. 59 and 61.

16. *Ibid.*, p. 9 and 90.

17. See V. Leroquais, *Le bréviaire de Philippe le Bon*, Bruxelles, 1929.

18. See L.J.M. Delaissé, *op. cit.*, p. 52; see also his *Miniature flamande: le Mécénat de Philippe le Bon*, Bruxelles, 1959, p. 182 ff.

19. A. W. Byvanck, *La Miniature dans les Pays-Bas septentrionaux*. Paris (Editions d'art et d'histoire) 1937, p. 72.

20. The fact that Vrelant who came from Utrecht introduced the Dutch style in Bruges is partially contested by J. D. Farquhar (see his *Creation and Imitation*, p. 29 ff).

21. A. W. Byvanck, *op. cit.*, p. 72.

22. See E. Mâle, *op. cit.*, p. 76.

23. Louis Réau, *Iconographie de l'art Chrétien*. Tome II. Iconographie de la Bible. II. Nouveau Testament, Paris (Presses Universitaires), 1957, p. 428.

24. See L.J.M. Delaissé, *op. cit.*, p. 74.

25. See L. Réau, *op. cit.*, pp. 452 and 453.

26. E. Mâle, *op. cit.*, p. 72.

27. F. Wilkinson, *Swords and daggers*. London (Blacks), 1967.

28. P. Martin, *Armour and Weapons*. London (H. Jenkins), 1967 (please note that 'Martin 215', for instance, refers to illustration, not page); see also the two very interesting chapters "Arms and armours in the middle ages" (pp. 97-123) on the development of arms and armours in the XVth century in Charles Boutell's *Arms and Armour*, London (Reeves and Turner), 1907.

29. M. Beaulieu and J. Baylé, *Le costume en Bourgogne* (1344-1477), Paris (P.U.F.) 1956.

30. W. Bruhn and M. Tilke, *A pictorial history of costume*, London (A. Zwemmer), 1955.

31. See E. Mâle, *op. cit.*, p. 371-2.

32. A. Harmand, *Jeanne d'Arc: son costume, son armure*, Paris (Leroux), 1929.

33. See A. Harmand, *op. cit.*, several refs.

34. E. Mâle. *op. cit.*, p. 371-2.

35. The coif worn by Mary in two miniatures has been discussed earlier.

36. See James Marrow, *"Circumdederunt me canes multi*: Christ's tormentors in Northern European Art of the late Middle Ages and the Early Renaissance" in *the Art Bulletin*, Vol. LIX number 2. June 1977. pp. 167-181.

37. *Ibid.*, p. 167.

38. See L. Réau, *op. cit.*, p. 434.

39. See E. Mâle, *op. cit.*, p. 27.

40. D. Miner, "Dutch illuminated Manuscripts in the Walters Art Gallery" in *The Connoisseur Yearbook* 1955. See pp. 66-7.

41. See E. Mâle, *op. cit.*, p. 73.

42. L. Réau, *op. cit.*, p. 514.

43. See G. Millet *Recherches sur l'iconographie de l'Evangile aux XIVe, XVe, et XVIe siècles*. Paris (Boccard) 1960, pp. 475-479.

44. See L. Réau, *op. cit.*, p. 523.

45. See E. Mâle, *op. cit.*, p. 26; this evolution is also discussed by G. Millet, *op. cit.*, pp. 502 ff.

46. See E. Mâle, *op. cit.*, p. 136.

47. Prof. R. Calkins at the *Manuscripta* Conference in St. Louis, October 1978.

48. See F. de Mély *"L'Histoire du bon roi Alexandre* du Musée Dutuit et les inscriptions de ses miniatures" in *Gazette des Beaux Arts*, 52e année (1910) 2e semestre pp. 173, 194. See also by the same: *Les primitifs et leurs signatures: Les Miniaturistes* 1913. Pp. 198-224.

49. See V. Leroquais, *op. cit.*, pp. 167-8.

50. *Le Beffroi*, Tome V, 1872 - 3, pp. 46-92 and 216 - 237.

51. See fol. 64v.

52. V. Leroquais, *op. cit.*, p. 154.

APPENDICES

Appendix A

The two additional stanzas in the Boston Manuscript
The text of the Passion ends identically in all three manuscripts:
"Que nos cuers en luy / Tiengne en union. Amen"

In the Boston Ms. this occurs in fol. 22v. Yet fol. 23 (the last one of the Ms.) shows, on the recto, two additional stanzas of a form and spirit completely alien to those of the Passion. Here they are:

> Arbre d'humaine nature
> En tant que ta nature dure
> Avise toy, le temps s'en va
> Il n'est arbre tant ait verdure
> Qu'en fin ne voist a pourriture
> Et jamais ne raverdira.
>
> Dame qui receustes l'ave
> Par lequel Dieu vous tint a mere
> Faittes que nous soyons lavé
> Des pechiez qui font mort amere.

The flight of time is the subject of the first stanza; a prayer to the Virgin that of the second: neither is very original. Human nature is compared to a tree which, in the end, does not become green again and rots. The prayer to the Virgin is even more disappointing. In a normal orison, there is a *sequitur* between the invocation and the request. Here, as an instance, is the collect for the eighth Sunday after Trinity:

> "O God whose never failing providence ordereth all things, both in heaven and earth: we humbly beseech thee to put away

> from us all hurtful things and to give us those things which be profitable for us."

Here the *sequitur* is Providence. But in the case of the second stanza, although the appearances are here: the invocation (*Dame*...) and the request (Faittes...) the *sequitur* is absent: there is no *sequitur* between the annunciation and the absolution form sin, unless the author meant to create one between *l'ave* and *lavé* which, at best, could be described as a poor pun on words.

It is most probable that these two stanzas are not by the author of the Passion and, in any case, they were certainly not meant to accompany the text, since neither the flight of time nor the need for absolution are relevant to the text. Moreover the defective line (*Arbre d'humaine nature* has 7 feet in a stanza of 8 feet lines) and the rather pedestrian images and metaphors are alien both to the style and the craft of the author of the Passion. In the absence of any evidence, how these stanzas came to be included remains a mystery.

Appendix B

Examples of double tercet in pentasyllabic lines in late mediaeval literature

The main circumstances surrounding the five XVth-century plays displaying double tercets in pentasyllabic lines are given here, together with samples of those lines.

1. *La vie et la Passion de Monseigneur Sainct Didier Martir et evesque de Lengres jouée en ladicte cité l'an 1482 composée par venerable et scientifique personne Maistre Guillaume Flamang chanoine de Lengres.* The text was edited by J. Carnandet from the only extant Ms. in the Chaumont public library; published in Paris by Techener in 1855.

Flamang was, according to various authorities, either from Flanders or from Langres. The play was performed in Langres by the *Confrérie des Pénitents*. It lasted three days and required 116 actors. The Saint was martyred either in 264 or in 451 and his relics were translated in 1315. This is, according to the editor (p.xxv), the story of a "martyr de la foi et de la charité".

P.98 eight pentasyllabic stanzas are given; Rhyme pattern aab/aab. In this passage we have a conversation between Didier on the one hand, and the bailiff and some burghers on the other. They welcome Didier at the town's gate:

> Le Bailly: Reverend Seigneur
> Plain de tout honneur
> Dieu vous doint sante! [...]
>
> Didier: Je croy que par moy
> La divine loy
> Sera maintenue.

Further on (p. 431) Lucifer indulges in a few astonishing lines on the same pattern:

> Corps, face et palpebre
> Boultez ou latebre
> De nostre delubre....etc...

2. *Le mistere de saint Quentin* was edited by Henri Chatelain in 1908 (Saint Quentin: Imprimerie Générale). The play was composed between 1460 or 1465 and 1492. Thus it is posterior to Arnould Gréban's *Passion* (1451); and it was retouched by Molinet. The place of the first performance is not known but it is recorded as having been performed on 14 November 1501 when Philippe, Archduke of Austria entered the city of Saint Quentin. The play is 24,000 lines long and took three or four days to perform. It has 150 speaking parts.

The following are examples of double tercets, and first, a dialogue between Marcellus and Dioclesien (lines 6998 - 7012):

> MARCELLUS
> Trop s'est ingeré
> Mais n'est si ferré
> Qui souvent ne glice.
>
> DIOCLESIEN
> Trop s'est amusé
> Qu'il ne s'est rusé
> Au fait ou se paine
>
> MARCELLUS
> Trop s'est abusé
> Mais mal avisé
> A souvent grant paine.
>
> DIOCLESIEN
> Veuilles vous vertir
> Et vous convertir
> Au port ou il flote.

MARCELLUS
Pour estre martir,
Jamais. Au partir
Fault conter a l'oste.

The next two examples are taken from dialogues between Rictiovaire and Quentin: (lines 7857 - 7886 display a great intensity of emotion):

RICTIOVAIRE
Tu és enchanteur,
De gens seducteur,
Par ton oeuvre immonde.

QUENTIN
Je suis serviteur
Du hault plasmateur
Qui forma le monde.

RICTIOVAIRE
Ceulx de mes escolles
Perdent leurs paroles
Par ta faulce envie.

QUENTIN
Prie tes ydoles
Que souvent acoles,
Qui leur rende vie.

RICTIOVAIRE
Se nos dieux ont lace.
Sans vuidier la place,
Tu mouras briefment.

QUENTIN
C'est vent de plouvace
De grosse menace
Petit vengement.

RICTIOVAIRE
Tu seras rataint,
Pendu ou estaint
Sans quelque dispense.

QUENTIN
Si seront tant maint,
Mais beaucop remaint
De ce que fol pense.

RICTIOVAIRE
Ton ame paillarde,
Fault qu'en enfer arde,
Ta vie l'appreuve.

> QUENTIN
> Mon Dieu me regarde
> Et qui bien se garde
> Tousjours bien se treuve.

(lines 11605 - 11616 display a comparable intensity):

> RICTIOVAIRE
> O Quentin, Quentin,
> Ton dieu celestin
> Te laisse au traveil.
>
> QUENTIN
> Tu scés, chien matin,
> Qu'aprés brum matin
> Luit le bel soleil.
>
> RICTIOVAIRE
> Maintenant apert
> Que ton corps se part,
> Car a la mort tent.
>
> QUENTIN
> Je n'en suis desert,
> Qui bon maistre sert
> Bon loyer attent.

3. *Le mystère des trois Doms* was edited by P.E. Giraud and Ul. Chevalier in 1887 at Lyon. The three "Doms" are the martyrs Séverin, Exupère and Félicien. The play was performed in the Franciscan church of Romans at Whitsun, 1509 (27, 28 and 29 May). It appears to have been written by Canon Pra. It has 11,289 lines which were to be performed over three days with a cast of 92.

There are quite a number of double tercets disseminated throughout the play, but the most poignant is perhaps the following (lines 8195 ff.); it should be noted that the rhyme here is aab / aab / bbc / bbc / ccd / ccd etc....

> Qui pourra soustiaire
> La dolante mere
> Si desolative? [...]
> Mort soys optative
> Pour moy nutritive
> Je t'en quiers de cueur.

Here is another example in the same vein (lines 8285 ff):

>Fault que le pas passe
>Fault que je trespasse
>Pour ceste nouvelle.
>Douleur me compasse
>Douleur me tient lasse
>Tant la sans rebelle....

It is noticeable that, in this play, it is always the *planctus* which is expressed in double tercets (lines 8491 ff):

>Sans avoir constance
>Mon cueur si se lance
>Au puys de tormant....etc...

4. *Le mystère de Saint Laurens* was edited by W. Söderhjelm and A. Wallensköld in 1890 at Helsingfors from a unique Gothic edition at the Bibliothèque Nationale, Paris. It was performed in 1460 at Chambéry: in 1467 at Compiège; in 1488 at Metz. The author is unknown. This apology of faith and Christian resignation has 8818 lines.

The double tercets are usually in rhymes of the type aab / aab / bbc / bbc etc...thus, lines 6543 ff:

>Mon Dieu souverains
>En mes faitz derrains
>Je te crie mercy.

Also lines 7925 ff:

>*In manus* te dy.
>Car droit a midy
>Le dis a ton pere
>Quant souffris pour my
>Le grant Vendredy
>Dure mort amere

In this play, as in the preceding one, it is the *planctus* which is expressed in this type of line.

5. I shall say very little of the *Mystère de la Passion* by Arnould Gréban as it is so well known. It was edited in 1878 by Gaston Paris and Gaston Raynaud. The double tercets are quite numerous in this play; the following 2 examples will serve as illustrations (lines 14077 ff):

>Je crie et sermonne,
>je prie et jargonne;
>j'ay beau sermonner,
>Je ne voy personne

And lines 26950 ff:
>qui son cuer adonne
>a me riens donner.
>
>Le cueur me remord
>de toy tenir mort,
>saint corps honoré,
>Qui pour nostre apport,
>salut et depport,
>as tant labouré.

Appendix C

Via Sacra, seu exercitum viae crucis dolorosae (...) Tyrnaviae 1763

This is the text of the *cantilena* used for moving from one station to the next. The service is discussed on pp. 105-106 *supra*.

1. Passionem Domini
   Recolamus pariter
   Fletu incessabili,
   Omnes unanimiter
   In vocibus
   Flebilibus
   Gemitibus
   Inenarrabilibus

2. In horto sequestratus
   Nocte obscurissima
   Orat patrem prostratus
   Prece secretissima
   Mox cruorem
   Cum horrore,
   Cum dolore
   Toto sudat pectore

3. Redit ad dormientes
   Pavidos discipulos
   Cernit appropinquantes
   Capitales aemulos;
   Ferus Judas
   Ducit turbas
   Furibundas
   Christi necis avidas.

4. Osculo salsissimo
   Capiendus traditur
   A Juda nequissimo
   Inimicis venditur;
   Christus Jesus
   Dire caesus
   Cruciandus
   Traditur tortoribus.

5. A suis discipulis
   Derelictus ducitur
   Velut latro vinculis
   Catenatus sistitur,
   Nequissimo
   Faevissimo,
   Ferissimo
   Caiphae illi pessimo.

6. Ad tribunal severum
   Judicandus sistitur
   Medius in luporum
   Collegio cernitur
   Stat mansuetus
   Dei Agnus
   Lacerandus
   Rabidorum morsibus.

7. Veritatis Authorem
   Onerant mendaciis,
   Faciem cum horrore
   Conspuunt spurcitiis
   Sanctissima
   In maxilla
   Fert alapsam
   Injuriosissimam.

8. Seductor proclamatur
   Commovisse populum
   Innocens judicatur
   Crucis ad patibulum
   Per immites
   Seniores,
   Pontifices
   Proceres et Judices.

9. Illusus induitur
   Vestibus ridiculis
   Lugubre proponitur
   Spectaculum populis
   Per publicas

   Urbis vias,
   Innumeras
   Patitur injurias.
10. Coeditur verberibus
   Multiplici vulnere,
   A suis tortoribus
   Tenero in corpore,
   Immaniter,
   Atrociter,
   Crudeliter,
   Immisericorditer.
11. Amictu purpureo
   Semi-nudus cingitur
   Infami ludibrio
   Ridendus exponitur,
   Vellunt comas,
   Caedunt genas,
   Spinas caput
   Sentit acutissimas.
12. Perfidi pontifices
   Cum insano populo
   Adsunt et carnifices
   Funebri spectaculo,
   Omnes clamant,
   Christum damnant,
   Ingeminant:
   Tolle, tolle, postulant.
13. Crucem poterat onustus
   Bene, gravi pondere,
   Figitur vulneratus
   Manu, pede, latere,
   In patulo
   Patibulo,
   A populo,
   Ridendus incredulo.
14. Eja, considerate
   Spectatores populi,
   Moribundum cernite
   Lachrymosi oculi;
   Sacrum ejus
   Tantum corpus
   Pallentibus
   Horridum livoribus.
15. Sociemur fideles
   Genitrici Mariae

    Conscedamus flebiles
    Ardua calvariae,
    Ad calcandas
    Crucis vias,
    Celebrandas
    Funebres Exequias.

16. Lugubrum Passionis
    Colendo memoriam
    Matrem compassionis
    Comitando Mariam;
    Per arduam
    Crucis viam,
    Reportandam
    Speramus victoriam.

17. Adoremus cernui,
    Trabe celsa pendulum,
    Observemus Dominum
    In tumulo conditum;
    Sacarum funus!
    Carum pignus!
    Pignoribus
    Cunctis pretiosius.

18. Jesu ! Fac participes
    Crucis et victoriae
    Supplices: Quod unum Te
    Comprecamur hodie!
    In vocibus
    Flebilibus
    Gemitibus
    Inenarrabilibus.

Appendix D

The 'Canticum Passionis'

The canticle of the Passion of our Lord appears in the *Processionarium* of the Dominicans, as well as in most Dominican Missals. I give here the rubrics in English in a somewhat abbreviated form, and the text in its complete Latin form, together with biblical identifications. I also give the music in the old square notation since, being extremely simple, it is unlikely to cause any problem in reading. This devotion is discussed on pp. 110-111.

Canticum de Passione Domini

This devotion is practised in many Religious Houses on Fridays in Lent and especially on Good Friday. The community is assembled, kneeling before the Crucifix. The cantor intones the first verse in the Second Tone in a subdued voice. Then each verse is sung, allowing an interval (lasting about the time of a Pater) for silent meditation. An inception is made at each verse.

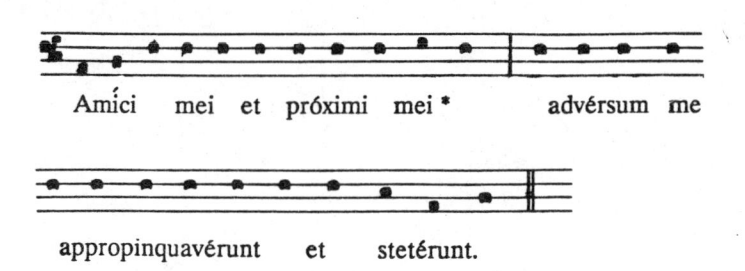

Amíci mei et próximi mei * advérsum me appropinquavérunt et stetérunt.

1. Amíci mei et próximi mei * advérsum me appropinquavérunt et stetérunt. (Ps. 37)

2. Traditus sum et non egrediebar: * oculi mei languerunt prae inopia. (Ps. 87)

3. Et factus est sudor meus * sicut guttae sanguinis decurrentis in terram. (Luke 22)

4. Circumdederunt me canes multi: * concilium malignantium obsedit me. (Ps. 21)

5. Corpus meum dedi percutientibus: * et genas meas vellentibus. (Isa. 50)

6. Faciem meam non averti ab increpantibus: * et conspuentibus in me. (Isa. 50)

7. Quoniam ego in flagella paratus sum: * et dolor meus in conspectu meo semper. (Ps. 37)

8. Milites plectentes coronam de spinis: * imposuerunt super caput meum. (Jo. 19)

9. Foderunt manus meas et pedes meos: * dinumeraverunt omnia ossa mea. (Ps. 21)

10. Et dederunt in escam meam fel: * et in siti mea potaverunt me aceto. (Ps. 68)

11. Omnes videntes me deriserunt me: * locuti sunt labiis et moverunt caput. (Ps. 21)

12. Ipsi vero consideraverunt et inspexerunt me: * diviserunt sibi vestiments mea, et super vestem meam miserunt sortem. (Ps. 21)

13. In manus tuas commendo spiritum meum: * redemisti me, Domine, Deus veritatis. (Ps. 30)

The choir repeats verse 13.

14. Memento famulorum tuorum, Domine: * dum veneris in regnum tuum. (Luke 23)

Then the cantor sings the following verse in a stronger voice:
15.

Jesus autem, emissa voce magna:* trá - didit spiritum. (Matt. 27)

After this verse, the Community pauses to meditate on the Passion of our Lord, then the Cantor continues on the 6th tone, with pauses as before:
16.

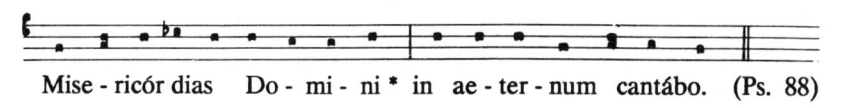

Mise - ricór dias Do - mi - ni * in ae - ter - num cantábo. (Ps. 88)

17. Vere languores nostros ipse tulit: * et dolores nostros ipse portavit. (Isa. 53)

18. Ipse autem vulneratus est propter iniquitates nostras: * attritus est propter scelera nostra. (Isa. 53)

19. Omnes nos quasi oves erravimus: * unusquisque in viam suam declinavit. (Isa. 53)

20. Et posuit in eo dominus: * iniquitates omnium nostrum. (Isa. 53)

21. Exsurge, quare obdormis, Domine? * exsurge, et ne repellas in finem. (Ps. 43)

The choir repeats verse 21; then the cantor repeats it again but on the following chant, which also serves for verse 22:

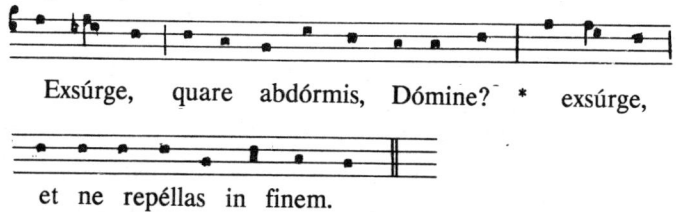

Exsúrge, quare abdórmis, Dómine? * exsúrge,

et ne repéllas in finem.

22. Ecce Deus Salvator meus: * fiducialiter agam et non timebo. (Isa. 12)

Then verse 23 is chanted as follows:

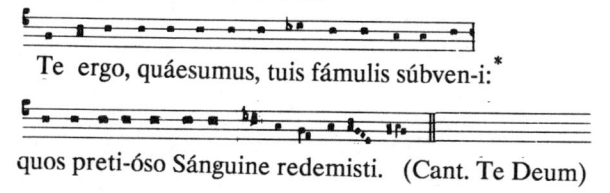

Te ergo, quáesumus, tuis fámulis súbven-i:*

quos preti-óso Sánguine redemisti. (Cant. Te Deum)

The Superior says:
    Miserere nostri, Jesu benigne.

The choir answers:
    Qui passus es clementer pro nobis.

The Superior says:
    Respice quaesumus Domine super hanc familiam tuam pro qua Dominus noster Jesus Christus non dubitavit manibus tradi nocentium: et Crucis subire tormentum.

omitting *qui tecum* etc., as during the whole of Holy Week.

There follows the Veneration of the Cross during which the hymn *Vexilla regis* is sung.

Appendix E

The Canticum Pindaricum loco *Te Deum* and the *Ode Saphica* [sic] *ad divam Catharinam*. See p. 113.

CANTICUM PINDARICUM loco TE DEUM

        Te nostra Deum musa canoris
        Laudat fidibus: teque fatetur
        Celi regem: terre Dominum.
        Cui dulcisonum fulgidus hymnum
        Chorus angelicus, concioque omnis
        Celicolarum concinit odas.
        Omnesque melos perdulce sonant
        Irrequietis motibus orbes.
        Tibi telluris serviat omnis
        Plaga: purpuream que vasta inter
        Jacet auroram: hesperiumque sinum. (*sic*)
        Et que gelidos ora triones
        Ac igniuomos arida soles
        Patitur: vel cerulee refluas
        Alluitur per Thetios undas.
        Nam nos stigii de fauce canis
        Eripuisti morte cruenta
        Et paradysi semper aphicum
        Quem primus homo perdidit hortum
        Nobis miseris restituisti.
        Hunc pie nobis largire Pater
        Per supplicium prolis amarum
        Et benedicte matris honestum
        Interventum atque omne piorum.
        Ingens meritum Christocolarum. Amen.

ODE SAPHICA (sic) AD DIVAM CATHARINAM

Virgo quam florens et aprica tellus
Fert ad Augustum speciosa Milum
Hic ubi surgunt. Macedum potentis
Menia regis.

a) only the upper end of the note appears in the original; an inadverdent omission;

b) the original reads DE, but this is clearly in error for CD which alone makes sense;

the chant is syllabic throughout, for all voices.

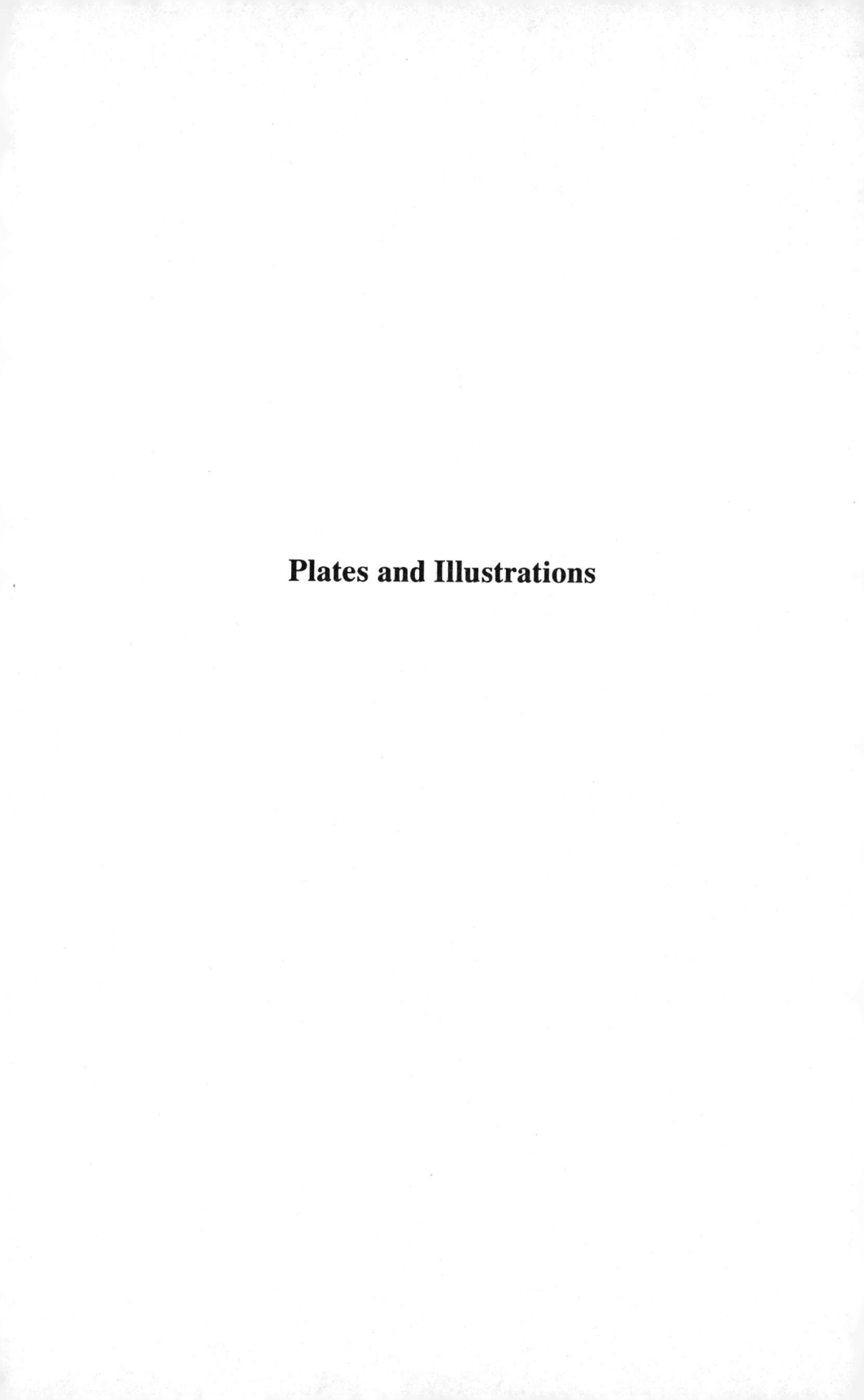

Plates and Illustrations

I. Boston Public Library Ms. 129: The Binding

II. Boston Public Library Ms. 129: fol. 1r.
The Betrayal in the Garden of Gethsemane

III. Boston Public Library Ms. 129: fol. 9r.
Jesus Before Pilate

IV. Boston Public Library Ms. 129: fol. 11r.
The Scourging of Jesus

V. Boston Public Library Ms. 129: fol. 13r.
Jesus Carrying his Cross

VI. Boston Public Library Ms. 129: fol. 15r.
Jesus dies on the Cross

VII. Boston Public Library Ms. 129: fol. 17r.
The Descent from the Cross

VIII. Boston Public Library Ms. 129: fol. 20v.
The Entombment

IX. Walters Art Gallery Ms. 439 fol. 28.

Illustration I. Young heads: (a) Judas (I); (b) Malchus (I); (c) John (V).

Illustration II. Old heads: (a) Pilate (II); (b) Nicodemus? (VI); (c) Joseph of Arimathaea? (VII); (d) Nicodemus? (VII).

Illustration III. Feet: (a) Soldier (I); (b) Soldier (II).

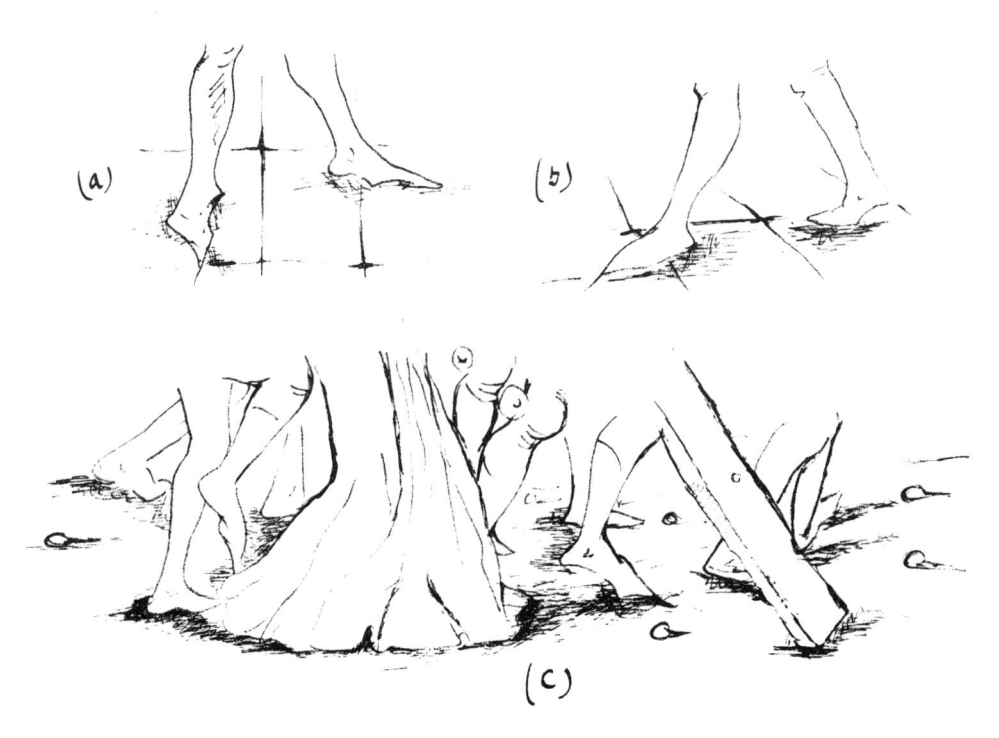

Illustration IV. Feet: (a) and (b) Varlets (III); (c) Soldiers (IV).

194

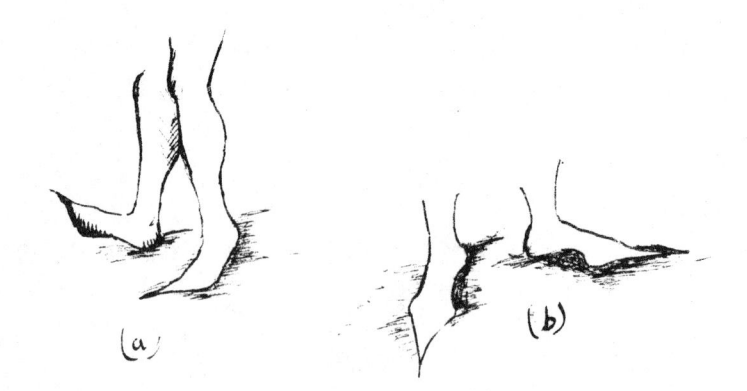

Illustration V. Feet: *Histoire du bon Roi Alexandre* Paris Collection Dutuit: Petit Palais. Ms. 456 (a) fol. 22; (b) fol. 63.

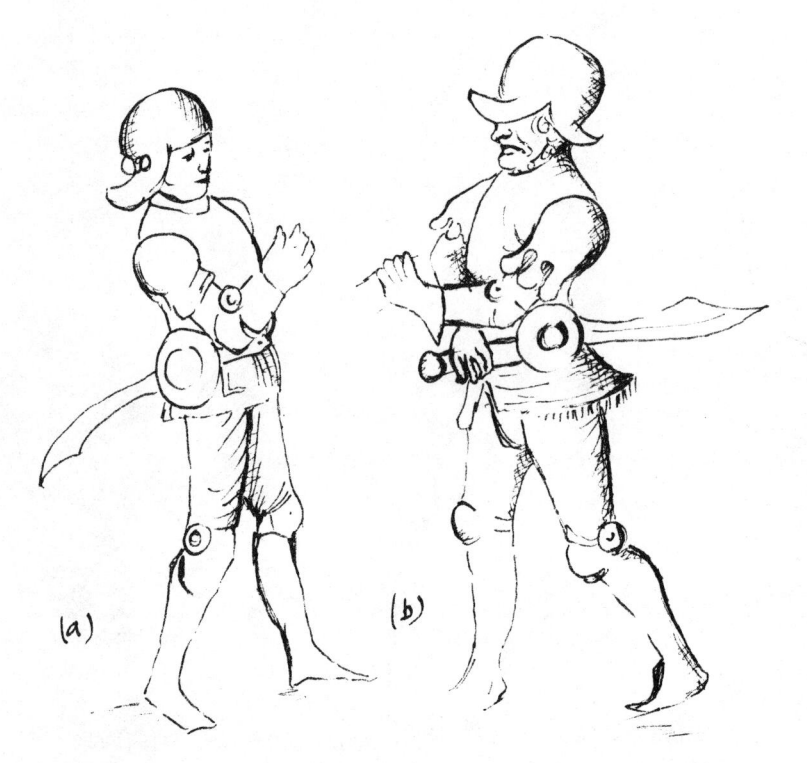

Illustration VI. Figures: (a) Soldier(II); (b) Soldier (I).

Illustration VII. Weapons: (a) miniature I; (b) miniature II; (c) miniature IV.

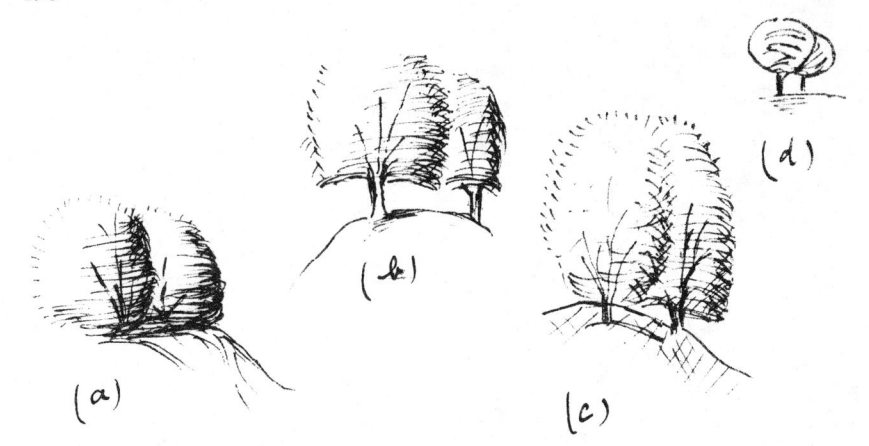

Illustration VIII. Trees: (a) miniature I; (b) miniature IV; (c) miniature VI; (d) miniature VI.

Illustration IX. Gestures: (a) St. Peter (I); (b) Varlet (II).

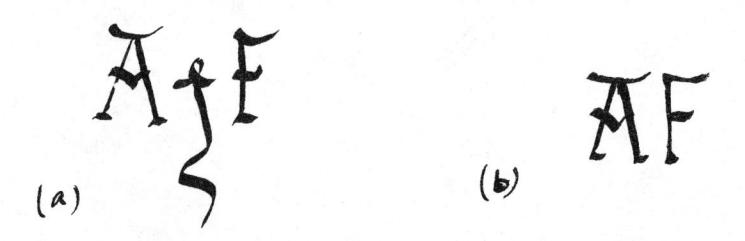

Illustration X. Signature: (a) Boston Public Library Ms. 129 fol. 1r; (b) Dutuit Collection Ms. 456 fol. 12.

Bibliography

Allgemeine deutsche Biographie. Leipzig, 1876.

Anderson, M. F., Jr. *Pierre Choinet, Le Livre des trois eages, édition critique et commentée.* Doctoral Dissertation: University of California, Davis, 1975.

Anglade, J. *Grammaire élémentaire de l'ancien français.* Paris (A. Colin), 1965.

Anselm (Pseudo). *Dialogus Beatae Mariae et Anselmi de Passione complete Domini.* Migne (ed.), P.L. 159.

Anselm of Laon. *Glossa Ordinaria.* Migne (ed.), P.L. 114.

Regula S. Augustini et Constitutiones FF. ordinis Praedictorum. Romae, 1690.

Beaulieu, M. and J. Baylé, *Le costume en Bourgogne* (1334-1477). Paris (P.U.F.), 1956.

Beaulieux, C. *Histoire de l'orthographe française.* Paris (Honoré Champion), 1967.

Bede (Ps). *De Meditatione Passionis Christi per septem diei horas libellus.*
Migne (ed.), P.L. 94.

Bibliographie nationale de Belgique. Bruxelles, 1881-3.

Bibliothèque nationale - Catalogue des manuscrits français: Ancien fonds. Tome I, Paris, 1868.

Birget, Saint. *Les Révélations célestes et divines de Sainte Brigitte de Suède communément appellée la chère espouse*, divisées en huit livres [...] Lyon (Simon Rigaud), ?1647.

Bonaventure, Saint. *Devotissimum opus passionis Christi Meditationum incipit: a seraphico doctore Bonaventura editum, omnibus predicatoribus devotisque religiosis necessarium nunc perrime impressum.* Venetiis (per Petrum de Quarengiis Bergomensem), Anno M. ccccc. XII. Die XX Kal. Martii.

_____. *Meditationes devotissimae totius vitae D.N.J.C. secundum S. Bonaventuram* [....] Lugduni (apud A. Gryphium), 1587.

Bonniwell, William R. *A History of the Dominican Liturgy*. New York (Joseph Wagner), 1944.

Boutell, Charles. *Arms and Armour*. London (Reeves and Turner), 1907.

Bragdon, C. *The Beautiful Necessity*. London n. d. (1st edition 1910).

Bruhn, W. and M. Tilke. *A Pictorial History of Costume*. London (A. Zwemmer), 1955.

Bukofzer, Manfred F. *Studies in Medieval and Renaissance Music*. London (Dent), 1951.

Burguy, G. F. *Grammaire de la langue d'oil* (Tomes I-III). Berlin (F. Schneider et cie), 1853-6.

Byvanck, A. W. *La Miniature dans les Pays-Bas septentrionaux*. Paris (Editions d'art et d'histoire), 1937.

Calkins, Robert G. *Distribution of labor: The illuminators of the Hours of Catherine of Cleves and their Workshop*. Philadelphia (The American Philosophical Society Philadelphia), August 1979.

_____. "Medieval and Renaissance illuminated manuscripts in the Cornell University Library." *The Cornell Library Journal* No. 13. May 1972.

Carnandet, J. *La vie et la Passion de Monseigneur Sainct Didier Martir et evesque de Lengres jouée en ladicte cité l'an 1482 composée par venerable et scientifique personne Maistre Guillaume Flamang chanoine de Lengres*. Paris (Techener), 1855.

Chatelain, Henri (ed.). *Le mistere de saint Quentin*. Saint Quentin (Imprimerie Générale), 1908.

_____. *Recherches sur le vers français au XVe siècle: rimes, mètres et strophes.* Paris (Champion), 1908.

Comestor, Petrus. *Historia Scholastica.* Migne (ed.), P.L. 198.

Constitutions of the Nuns of the Sacred Order of Preachers[...](Vatican Press), 1930.

Cornelius a Lapide. *Comm. on Matt.* XXVII, 15. Antwerp ed. 1732.

Cotgrave, R. *A Dictionarie of the French and English Tongues* [...]London, 1611.

Curtius, Cornelius. *De clavis Dominicis Liber*[...] Antwerp, 1670.

Daly, Lowrie J. *Benedictine Monasticism.* New York, n. d.

Dauzat, A.*(et al) Nouveau dictionnaire étymologique.* Paris (Larousse), 1964.

Delaissé, L.M.J. *A Century of Dutch Manuscript Illumination.* Berkeley (UCLA Press), 1968.

_____. *La Miniature flamande*: *le Mécénat de Philippe le Bon.* Bruxelles, 1959.

Devaux, Y. *Dix siècles de reliure,* Paris (Pygmalion), 1977.

Dictionary of American Biography.

Dionysius Areopagita. *Opera.* Migne (ed.), P.G. 111

Duriez, Georges. *La Théologie dans de drame religieux en Allemagne au moyen âge.* Lille (*Mémoires et Travaux publiés par les Professeurs des Facultés Catholiques de Lille*), 1914.

Elcock, W.D. *The Romance Languages.* London (Faber and Faber), 1960.

Farquhar, J. D. *Creation and Imitation.* New York (Nova/NYIT University Press), 1976.

Fisher, C. (ed.) *Die 'Meditationes Vitae Christi'* [....]*AFH*, t. 25, 1932.

Flutre, . F. *Le Moyen Picard d'après les textes littéraires du temps (1560-1660).* Amiens (Société de linguistique picarde), 1970.

Fouché, P. *Morphologie historique du français. Le Verbe.* Paris (Klincksieck), 1967.

Foulet, A. and Speer, M. B. : *On Editing Old French Texts.* R.P.K. Lawrence, 1979.

Foulet, L. *Petite syntaxe de l'ancien français.* Paris (Champion), 1967.

Franck, G. (ed.) *Le Livre de la Passion.* Paris (CFMA), 1930.

Froger, J. *La critique des textes et son automatisation.* Paris (Dunod), 1968.

Gastoué, Amédée. *Le Cantique populaire en France.* Lyon (Janin), 1924.

_____. *Variations sur la musique d'Eglise.* Paris (Schola), 1913.

Giraud, P.E. and Ul. Chevalier (eds.) *Le Mystère des trois Doms.* Lyon, 1887.

Godefroy, Frederic. *Dictionnaire de l'ancienne langue française.* Paris (Vieweg), 1881-1902; New York Kraus Reprint, 1961.

Gossen, C. T. *Grammaire de l'Ancien Picard.* Parie (Klincksieck), 1970.

Grandsaignes d'Hauterive, R. *Dictionnaire d'ancien français, Moyen Age et Renaissance.* Paris (Larousse), 1947.

Greene, R.L. *The Early English Carols.* Oxford (Clarendon), 1935.

Greimas, A. J. *Dictionnaire de l'ancien français jusqu 'au milieu du XIVe siècle.* Paris (Larousse), 1968

Groves's Dictionary of Music and Musicians (5th edition). London (Macmillan's), 1954.

Hamilton, George H. and D.V. Thompson (eds.) *De Arte illuminandi.* New Haven (Yale University Press), 1933.

Harmand, A. *Jeanne d'Arc: son costume, son armure.* Paris (Leroux), 1929.

Harrison, Frank Ll. *Music in Medieval Britain.* London (Kegan Paul), 1958.

Hefele, Charles Joseph. *Histoire des Conciles.* Paris (Letouzey), 1916.

Hekelius, Josef-Frederik. *Dessertatio historico-philologico-theologica de habitu regio, Christo in Passione a Judeis, in ignominiam, oblato.* Chemnitz, 1675.

Henry, A. *Wallon et Wallonie.* Bruxelles (La Renaissance du Livre), 1974.

Huguet, E. *Dictionnaire de la langue française du seizième siècle.* Paris. (Champion-Didier), 1925-1967.

Jeanroy, Alfred. *Les origines de la poésie lyrique en France au moyen-âge.* Paris (Champion), 1904.

John Chrysostom (Ps). *Opera.* Migne (ed.), P.G. Vol. 62. Tome 11.

Jordan-Stallings, M. (ed.) *Meditationes Vitae Christi.* Ilkley (Scholar Press), 1978.

Langlois, Ernest. *Recueil d'arts de seconde rhétorique.* Documents inédits sur l'histoire de France, série 5, vol. 8. Paris (Imprimerie Nationale), 1902.

Le Beffroi, Tome V, 1872-3.

Leroquais, V. *Le brévaire de Philippe le Bon.* Bruxelles, 1929.

_____. *Un Livre d'heures manuscrit à l'usage de Mâcon.* Mâcon, 1935.

Lote, George, *Histoire du vers français.* Paris (Hatier), 1955.

Ludolph of Saxony. *Vita Christi.* Venetis (apud Guerrero Fratres et Franciscum Zilletum), 1581.

Mâle, E. *L'art religieux de la fin du moyen âge en France.* Paris (A. Colin), 1925.

Maillard, O. *Chanson piteuse composée par frère Olivier Maillard en pleine prédication au son de la chanson nommée "Bergeronnette Savoisienne" et chantée à Toulouse environ la Penthecouste par ledit Maillard, lui estant en chaire de prédication, l'an mil cinq cens et deux. Et bien tost apres trespassa.* s.l., ?1502.

Marrow, James. *"Circumdederunt me canes multi*: Christ's tormentors in Northern European Art of the late Middle Ages and the Early Renaissance." *The Art Bulletin,* Vol. LIX No. 2. June 1977.

Martin, H. *Les Miniaturistes français.* Paris (Henri Leclerc), 1906.

Martin, P. *Armour and Weapons.* London (H. Jenkins), 1967.

Marzac, N. *Richard Rolle de Hampole, 1300-1349. Vie et oeuvres suivies du Tractatus super apocalypsim, Texte critique avec traduction et commentaire*[...] Paris (Librairie Philosophique Vrin), 1968.

_____. *Robert Ciboule Edition critique du sermon "Qui Manducat me*"[....]Cambridge (MHRA), 1971.

Mattesini, Francesco. *Le Origini del Terz'Ordine Francescano.* Milano, n. d.

Mély, F. de. "*L'Histoire du bon roi Alexandre* du Musée Dutuit et les inscriptions de ses miniatures." *Gazette des Beaux* Arts, 52e année (1910).

_____. *Les primitifs et leurs signatures, Les Miniaturistes,* s.l. 1913.

Millet, G. *Recherches sur l'iconographie de l'Evangile aux XIVe, XVe et XVIe siècles.* Paris (Boccard), 1960.

Miner, D. "Dutch Illuminated Manuscripts in the Walters Art Gallery." *The Connoisseur Yearbook*, 1955.

Moreau, E.: *Histoire de l'Eglise en Belgique,* vol. IV Bruxelles, *1947.*

Opuscules complets de St.François d'Assise [...] par le traducteur des oeuvres de Catherine Emmerich. Tournai, 1864.

Panofski, E. *Early Netherlandish Painting.* Cambridge Mass., 1960.

Paris, P. *Les manuscrits français de la bibliothèque du Roi.* Paris, 1838.

Paris, G. and G. Raynaud. (eds.) *Le Mystère de la Passion d'Arnould Gréban.* 1878.

Petrus Comestor. *Historia Scholastica.* Migne (ed.) P. L. 198.

Pirenne, H. *Histoire de Belgique.* vol. II, Bruxelles (Henri Lamertin), 1908.

Pope, M. K. *From Latin to Modern French.* Manchester (U. P. Manchester), 1934.

Praet, O. van. *Recherches sur Louis de Bruges.* Paris, 1831.

Rapp, Francis: "FRANCE: le 15e. siècle", in M. Viller, (ed.) *Dictionnaire de Spiritualité* [...]. Paris (Beauchesne), 1953.

Réau, Louis. *Iconographie de l'art chrétien.* Tome II. Iconographie de la Bible. II Nouveau Testament. Paris (Presses Universitaires), 1957.

Reinmann, Gerald Joseph. *The Third Order of St. Francis*, Studies in Canon Law No. 50. Washington D. C. (Catholic University of America), 1928.

Remacle, L. *Le problème de l'ancien wallon.* Liège (BFPLUL), 1948.

――――――. *Syntaxe du parler wallon de la Gleize.* Liège (BFPLUL), 1956.

Ripabottoni, Alessandro de: *I fratelli laici nel primo ordine francescano.* Rome, 1956.

Robbins, R. H. "The Earliest Carols and the Franciscans." *Modern Language Notes*, vol. 53, No. 4. April 1938.

Schlichterus, C.L. *Observatio de alba Christi veste, ad Luc. XXVII v. 2.* Bremen, 1732.

Seton, Walter W. (ed.) *Two Fifteenth-century Franciscan Rules.* London (EETS), 1914.

Smith, M. Teasdale. "The use of grisaille as a lenten obvservance." *Marsyas* vol. VIII, 1957-1959.

Söderhjelm, W. and A. Wallensköld (eds.) *Les mystère de Saint Laurens.* Helsingfors, 1890.

Sonet, Jean. *Répertoire d'incipit de prières en ancien français.* Genève (Droz), 1956.

Stiennon, J. *Paléographie du Moyen Age.* Paris (A. Colin), 1966.
Thompson, David V. *The materials and techniques of medieval painting.* New York (Dover Publications), 1956.
Tischendorf, C. (ed.) *Evangelia Apocrypha.* Leipzig, 1853.
Tobler A. *Altfranzösisches Wörterbuch.* Berlin (Weidmannsche Buchhandlung), 1925-1960.
Tolnay, C. de. *Le Maître de Flémalle.* Bruxelles, 1939.
Venantius-à-Lisle-en-Rigault, Rmus P. (ed.) *Monumenta ad Constitutiones Ordinis Fratrum Minorum Capuccinoruum pertinenta.* Romae (Curia Generalitia), 1916.
Voragine, J. de. *Legenda Aurea,* any edition.
Wallis, N. de. *Eléments de paléographie.* Paris, 1838.
Walters Art Gallery. *Illuminated Books of the Middle Ages and the Renaissance.* Baltimore, 1949.
_____. *The International Style: The Arts in Europe around 1400.* Baltimore, Fall 1962.
Wartburg von, Walter. *Französisches etymologisches Wörterbuch.* 1948.
Wilkinson, F. *Swords and daggers.* London (Blacks), 1967.
Wilmet, M. *Le système de l'indicatif en moyen français.* Genève (Droz), 1970.

Index Nominum

This Index of Names is selective: it contains only those names which, in the various commentaries, make a significant contribution to the understanding of the text. It has been deemed unnecessary to establish an Index of Subjects as each section of the commentary is self-contained.

A

Ambrose, St., 78
Annas, 7, 22, 74, 75, 123
Anselm, Ps., 81, 82, 83, 85, 86, 87, 146
Aubert, D., 34, 35
Augustine, St., 89

B

Barabbas, 71
Bede, Ps., 76, 81, 83
Bede, Ven., 105
Benton, J.H. vi, 33
Birget, St., 78, 79, 80, 81, 150
Bonaventure, Ps. viii, 31, 69, 71, 72, 80, 83, 85, 87, 89, 179
Borsele, Marguerite de 30
Bougerol, J.G. viii, 29, 30, 31, 34, 148, 149
Bruges, Louis de viii, 29, 30, 31, 34, 148, 149
Bukofzer, M., 108
Bywanck, A.W., 144

C

Caiaphas, 7, 22, 75
Calkins, R., 143
Catherine of Cleves, Master of, 125
Catherine, St., 110
Celtis, C., 111
Chatelain, H., 49, 52, 56, 57, 164
Chrysostom, Ps., 85
Cornelius a Lapide, 77
Corvin, L., 111, 179

D

Daly, L. J., 101
Debongnie, P., 97

Delaissé, L.M.J., 35, 132, 135, 136, 141, 143
Denis, St., 15, 25, 88
Dionysius, Areopagite, 88
Duquesne, J., 34
Duriez, G., 73, 74, 82
Dutuit, Coll., 35, 134, 154, 194, 197

F

Fieret, A., 154
Flanders (*also* Flemish), 92, 131, 132, 143, 144, 145, 151
Fontaines, A. de 154
Fraet, A. ix, 155
Francis, St. (Second Rule of), 100, 103, 104
Froger, J., viii, 37

G

Gastoué, A., 106-107, 108
Gerard de Groote, 92
Gerlac Peters, 92
Gerson, J., viii
Greban, A., 49, 52, 167
Greene, R.L., 109-110

H

Harrison, F. Ll., 109
Herod, 10, 23, 77
Holkham Hall (Library), 35, 143, 146

J

Jesus *passim*
John, St. (*also* Gospel of), 71, 73, 74, 78, 79, 86, 89, 90, 123, 127, 128, 129, 130, 133, 137, 152, 153, 193

Joseph of Arimathaea, 17, 25, 86, 89, 91, 128, 129, 133, 140, 149, 151, 152, 193
Judas, 6, 22, 71, 73, 74, 75, 122, 133, 135, 150

L

Langlois, E., 50, 51, 56
Leroquais, V., 142, 154, 155
Le Tavernier, 131
Longin, 16, 85, 86, 88, 89
Lote, G., 52, 55
Ludolf of Saxony, 72, 77, 80, 83, 85, 87, 89, 105
Luke, St. (Gospel of), 71, 83

M

Maillard, O., 108
Malchus, 73, 74, 82, 122, 133, 135, 136, 150, 153, 193
Male, E., 87, 138, 145, 146, 149, 150, 151, 152, 153
Mark, St. (Gospel of), 76, 90
Marrow, J., 150
Martin, P., 147, 148, 149
Mary, Virgin, 15, 16, 17, 18, 25, 26, 70, 79, 80, 81, 85, 86, 87, 88, 89, 90, 91, 110, 114, 127, 128, 129, 130, 137, 139, 140, 141, 146, 152, 153, 161
Matthew, St. (Gospel of), 73, 76, 78, 79, 88, 123
Miélot, J., 148
Millet, G., 151
Molinet, J., 50, 51, 55
Moreau, E., ix

N

Nicodemus (and Gospel of), 17, 25, 84, 85, 86, 89, 91, 96, 128, 129, 133, 140, 149, 151, 152, 153, 193

P

Paul, St. (Ep.), 84
Peter, St., 71, 73, 74, 75, 83, 122, 137

Picard (*also* Picardy), viii, 50, 57, 58, 61, 62, 63, 64, 92
Pierre de Blois, 74
Pilate, 9, 11, 23, 77, 79, 123, 124, 136, 149
Pilate (Acts of), 88, 96, 137, 139
Protagoras, 170

R

Rapp, F., ix
Reaney, G., 118
Réau, L., 145, 150, 151, 152
Robbins, R.H., 109

S

Sabatier, P., vi
Samblanx, C. de, 34
Simeon, 91
Simon of Cyrene, 79

T

Thomas à Kempis, 92

V

Veronica, 80
Villon, 70
Vrelant, G., ix, 134, 136, 142, 143, 144, 154, 155

W

Walloon, viii, 61, 62
Walters Art Gallery, 140, 141, 143, 144, 145, 146, 150, 151, 192
Wilkinson, F., 146, 147

MEDIAEVAL STUDIES

1. Edelgard E. DuBruck (ed.), **New Images of Medieval Women: Essays Toward a Cultural Anthropology**
2. M. Kilian Hufgard, **Saint Bernard of Clairvaux: A Theory of Art Formulated From His Writings and Illustrated in Twelfth-Century Works of Art**
3. Nancy van Deusen (ed.), **Paradigms in Medieval Thought Applications in Medieval Disciplines: A Symposium**
4. Nicole Crossley-Holland (ed.), **A Fifteenth-Century Franciscan French Office: Translation and Commentary of the** *Hours of the Passion*
5. P. Ranft, **The Function of Monasticism in the High Middle Ages**
6. Ian Thompson and Louis Perraud, **Ten Latin Schooltexts of the Middle Ages: Translated Selections**
7. William L. Urban, **Dithmarschen, A Medieval Peasant Republic**
8. Elizabeth Mary McNamer, **The Education of Heloise: Methods, Content, and Purpose of Learning in the Twelfth-Century**